JOURNEYS WITH THE PEOPLE OF GENESIS

Journeys
with the
People
of
Genesis

*Contemporary Insights
from the Old Testament*

JAMES A. HARNISH

UPPER
ROOM BOOKS
NASHVILLE

JOURNEYS WITH THE PEOPLE OF GENESIS

Copyright © 1989 James A. Harnish. All rights reserved.

No part of this book may be reproduced in any manner whatsoever without written permission of the publisher except in brief quotations embodied in critical articles or reviews. For information, address The Upper Room, 1908 Grand Avenue, P.O. Box 189, Nashville, Tennessee 37202.

Scripture quotations designated RSV are from the Revised Standard Version of the Bible, copyrighted 1946, 1952, and © 1971 by the Division of Christian Education, National Council of Churches of Christ in the United States of America, and are used by permission.

Scripture quotations designated TEV are from the *Good News Bible, The Bible in Today's English Version,* copyright by American Bible Society, 1966, 1971, © 1976, and are used by permission.

Scripture quotations designated KJV are from the King James Version of the Bible.

Scripture quotations not otherwise identified are the author's paraphrase.

Excerpt from "Blowin' in the Wind" by Bob Dylan, © 1962 WARNER BROS. INC. All rights reserved. Used by permission.

Excerpts from *Peculiar Treasures* by Frederick Buechner, © 1979 Frederick Buechner, Harper & Row, Publishers, Inc. Used by permission.

Excerpt from I HAVE A DREAM by Martin Luther King, Jr., reprinted by permission of Joan Daves. Copyright © 1963 by Martin Luther King, Jr.

"Stubborn Ounces" is reprinted from SIGNATURE: NEW AND SELECTED POEMS, by Bonaro Overstreet, by permission of W. W. Norton & Company, Inc. Copyright © 1978 by W. W. Norton & Company, Inc.

Excerpt from THE NEW BEING by Paul Tillich reprinted by permission of Charles Scribner's Sons, an imprint of Macmillan Publishing Company. Copyright 1955 Paul Tillich; renewed © Hannah Tillich.

Excerpt from LETTERS AND PAPERS FROM PRISON, Enlarged Edition, by Dietrich Bonhoeffer reprinted with permission of Macmillan Publishing Company and SCM Press, Ltd. Copyright © 1953, 1967, 1971 by SCM Press, Ltd.

Book Design: John Robinson
Cover Design: David Weilmeunster
First Printing: April 1989 (7)
Library of Congress Catalog Card Number: 88-051471
ISBN: 0-8358-0590-5

PRINTED IN THE UNITED STATES OF AMERICA

*In gratitude for my parents,
whose life of faith was the beginning of my own*

CONTENTS

Introduction		9
One	Creation, Fall, and Then What?	15
Two	The Rainbow Connection	23
Three	Acting on the Promises	33
Four	Strangely Blessed	41
Five	Learning to Laugh with God	47
Six	The Road to Mount Moriah	57
Seven	If You Don't Do It . . .	67
Eight	Wrestling in the Dark, Limping Toward the Dawn	77
Nine	The Best Thing About Growing Old	89

Ten	Don't Forget Joseph	*95*
Eleven	Here Comes the Dreamer!	*101*
Twelve	The Power to See It Through	*109*
Thirteen	How God Turns Evil into Good	*119*

INTRODUCTION

I poured myself a cup of coffee and settled down on the reception room sofa to wait my turn to be interviewed on the local "talk" radio station. From overhead speakers I could hear the voices of two women discussing divorce and spouse abuse in central Florida. It was a grueling recital of the tragedy of marital conflict, climaxed by the true story of the husband who informed his wife, "All you really need is a good beating," and proceeded to give her one.

Before breaking for the eight o'clock news headlines, the show's hostess joked, "Well, we have a minister on next. I can't wait to see what he has to say to all of this!"

The guests changed places, and after a commercial for a local car dealer, she opened the interview with this question: "You say you are a believer, but how can you believe in something you can't see?" That question was followed in rapid-fire succession with questions from the hostess and the listeners revolving around these themes: How can you believe in a good God in such an evil world? Why does God permit spouse abuse, hunger, AIDS, or war? How can you talk about credible Christian faith with the obvious corruption of the televangelists and the demise of religious leaders in the news almost every day?

They were all sincere, though unoriginal, questions that have been and continue to be asked by disciples and doubters, saints and skeptics, bedrock believers and confirmed agnostics. We are all on common ground here.

I had barely begun to respond to the questions when we were interrupted for a special news bulletin. An unidentified gunman had opened fire in a shopping center parking lot in the quiet town of Palm Bay, just an hour's drive from Orlando. At least a dozen people had been shot, several were confirmed dead, and the gunman was holding others hostage in the supermarket. Suddenly the calls and the questions took on an immediacy we had not sensed before. These were no longer theoretical questions, but honest cries from the soul in response to the unfolding tragedy in the news bulletins.

The station manager canceled the scheduled programming and we stayed on the air until midnight, attempting to put a theological and moral framework around a gruesome portrait of human suffering.

Looking back on the experience, I realized again that it is not enough to find, in the words of a recent automobile sales pitch, "something to believe in." Theology makes a difference. The character of the God in whom we place our faith and the content of the spiritual affirmations upon which we build our lives are critically important, particularly when we face difficult, confusing, or painful times.

A fifteen-year-old boy from our youth group, a day-brightener of the first rank, one of my elder daughter's best friends, was killed instantly in a senseless car accident last spring. When our youth minister announced that the church would be open for sharing the next evening, over two hundred youths from across the community appeared. The time was filled with honest emotion and genuine expressions of laughter, friendship, and tears. But one young man whom none of us knew said something that deeply disturbed me. He told the group that his pastor comforted him by saying that God walks through the garden of life and plucks the finest flowers to take back to heaven.

My immediate reaction was, How could anyone with any modicum of good sense believe that? How could you trust or love a God like that? It was for me a tragic example of the effects of a well-intentioned but implausible image of God.

Theology matters. The character of the God in whom we believe makes a gigantic difference in how we respond to the real experiences of life.

This is a book about faith—the kind of daring faith that can survive in difficult times. It is also about God—the kind of God who is revealed in what B. W. Anderson called *The Unfolding Drama of the Bible*, the kind of God who is fit to love and worthy of trust. This is also a book about people—the kind of people who must claim their faith in a world where it is not always easy or comfortable to believe, a world where we find ourselves inextricably enmeshed in the tangle of good and evil, truth and falsehood, joy and pain. It is an attempt to deal honestly with what it means for people like us to find a vital relationship with the living God that takes seriously the real world in which we live.

The setting for our thinking is the Old Testament Book of Genesis. The title means "beginning." The first book in the Bible is a marvelous collection of stories about the beginning of the family of faith. The thread holding their stories together is their common experience with the living God.

But there is more. Each of these people dared to live by faith in difficult times. In their unique situations they faced circumstances and conflicts that contradicted their faith. Although these stories were told and retold for centuries, they probably emerged in their written form during the exile, composed in the caldron of human suffering, a shout of hope against the darkness that had engulfed the children of Israel.

Reliving the tales of these people is like going to an old-fashioned family reunion. The entire clan is there; the picnic tables are weighted down with the aunts' favorite recipes; the cousins are running around all over the place. After the meal is consumed and the tablecloths are spread across the remaining dishes to protect them until suppertime, we settle down in our lawn chairs and someone asks, "Whatever happened to . . . ?" The wheels begin to turn; the stories begin to flow; we hear the familiar tales of our family history. We go home in the evening stronger persons because we know more fully who we are.

The writer of the New Testament Letter to the Hebrews was like an elder uncle who encouraged his readers for the difficult times they faced by retelling the stories of Abraham and Sarah, Isaac and Rebecca, Jacob and Esau, and Joseph. The writer concluded with these words: "What a record all of these have won by their faith! Yet they did not receive what God had promised, because . . . His purpose was that only in company with us would they be made perfect" (Heb. 11:39-40, TEV).

These are not merely ancient stories collected and retold out of a dusty past. Like Uncle Elwood's stories at the family reunions, they are the stories through which we discover who we are and from which we find strength,

INTRODUCTION

encouragement, and hope for the living of our days. The drama of faith will never be complete until we discover in the present the same daring faith our forebears experienced in the past, until we find God's presence in our world.

How can you believe in a God you can't see? How can you continue to believe in a good God in what sometimes appears to be a bad world? As a person of faith, how do you reconcile your trust in a creative God with the harsh facts of the day and time in which we live?

I take great comfort in knowing that I am not the first or last person to ask those questions. As I wrestle with them I am standing in the long line of the people of the covenant, men and women who have known the same searing pain, the same penetrating doubt, the same confusing contradictions, but who have dared to affirm the goodness, love, and faithfulness of the God revealed to us first in the book of beginnings and ultimately in Jesus Christ.

Author and essayist Madeleine L'Engle was among a group of writers, theologians, and professors who were asked to share with the readers of *The Christian Century* what book had been most influential to them in the past year. She responded:

> There is no question that the book that has been most influential for me this past year is the Bible's first one: Genesis. . . .
>
> The marvelous story of the Creation is for me filled with incredible joy . . . the Word shouting all things into being in a great cry of joy.
>
> Genesis is also filled with marvelous people—flawed and human—and underlines for me that God does not choose "qualified" people to do the Work of Love. . . .
>
> Genesis has everything—all the human vices and glories, love and lust, hatred, murder, sacrifice, and a great story. There is no end to plumbing its depths.

JOURNEYS WITH THE PEOPLE OF GENESIS

Although this book is no attempt to plumb the depths of the Book of Genesis, it is not too much for me to hope that the retelling of these stories will enable each of us to discover, as the exiled Israelites did, a daring faith that can answer the question, Where in the world is God?

CHAPTER ONE

Creation, Fall, and Then What?

Such welcome and unwelcome things at once
'Tis hard to reconcile.
—William Shakespeare

READ GENESIS 1–5

Where does it all begin—this story of who and what I am? Should I take you to a college town in western Pennsylvania and a now nonexistent frame house on Grand Avenue that I first remember as home? Should I describe the house on Wood Street with the green canvas awnings that now has a stranger's name on the mailbox?

Perhaps I should go back a generation and take you to the "old stone house" where my paternal grandparents settled, labored, lived, and died, or to the miniscule coal mining village of Ramsey and the one-room church where my grandmother took her seven children, each with a penny for the offering if the family had an income that week.

Perhaps that is not far enough. I could go behind them

to the Alexanders immigrating from Ireland during the potato famine, or a Roman Catholic priest in Germany who suddenly renounced his vows and left for America for reasons no one has ever been able to explain.

Where does it all begin—this story of who and what we are?

Deep in our souls we know that we are not telling the whole story, even when we trace our ancestry across all the genetic lines of our forebears. Beneath the racial, cultural, historical, and biological factors that make us so different from one another, there is a deeper human identity, impossible to explain, but equally impossible to deny. Back there in the shrouded generations long dead is the land of our beginning, the place where we discover who we were created to be. It is there that we begin to discover the character of the God who the biblical writers dared to believe was active in human history.

The Genesis storytellers begin where all our human stories begin, with the drama of the birth of the world, the first knife strokes of the master sculptor in the chaotic clay of creation: "In the beginning God created the heavens and the earth" (1:1, RSV).

I suspect that across the centuries there has been more damage done to this passage of scripture by its friends than by its enemies. At least that seems to be the case in the latter half of the 1980s, as well-intentioned fundamentalists attempt to resurrect the Scopes Monkey Trial in the battle over creationism in the public schools. As I watch the struggle unfold, I find two tragic ironies. The first is that today more and more scientists are affirming details in the study of the origin of the universe that lead directly toward faith in God.

I met an astrophysicist and church member for lunch in a local restaurant. I listened in awe as he described discoveries about the structure of the atom that have the potential of turning our whole understanding of matter in a new direction. He concluded by sharing how his study has encouraged his growing faith in God.

After listening to concepts that stretched my sophomoric brain to its limits—I had barely survived Dr. Westerfield's beginning astronomy course in college!—I told him about an article in *The Christian Century* by Holmes Rolston III entitled "Shaken Atheism: A Look at the Fine-Tuned Universe." In this article the Colorado State University professor describes the recent discoveries of astrophysicists and microphysicists about the precise design by which the world came into being. He quotes astronomer Fred Hoyle whose atheism was shaken by his own discovery that in the stars, carbon just manages to form and then just avoids complete conversion into oxygen. If one atomic level had varied .5 percent, life would have been impossible. Wrote Hoyle, "A common sense interpretation of the facts suggests that a superintellect has monkeyed with the physics. . . . The numbers one calculates from the facts seem to me so overwhelming as to put this conclusion almost beyond question." The scientific approach that some Christians seem so intent to deny is leading others to a deeper faith.

The second irony is that the Bible was never intended to be a scientific text on the origin of the universe. It is a book of faith in the God of creation. The Old Testament poets were not attempting to answer the question of *how* the world came into being; their concern was with *why* it is here and *who* did it.

The opening words of the Bible are the poetry of faith, the joyful cry of the soul to the God who brings order out of chaos, who speaks forth creation.

"Let there be light"—and the light appeared and God was pleased. "Let the waters be separated"—and it was done. "Let the land appear"—and it was done. "Let lights appear in the sky"—and they appeared. "Let the water be filled with many kinds of living beings and let the air be filled with birds"—and God was pleased with all the creatures. "Let the earth produce all kinds of animal life"—and it was done.

Here is a picture of the God who calls creation out of chaos, who rejoices in the infinite variety of the species, who celebrates the riot of color, the cacophony of sound, the dazzling spectacle of the natural order. The Genesis narrative is a hymn of adoration to the God who longed so much for companionship that one of the creatures was formed in God's own image, entrusted with wisdom, insight, and freedom; gifted with the capacity for love, the ability to think, even the power to create new life. And when God saw it all, God said that it was very good.

The writer of Genesis describes the God who looks on the first dawn of creation not as a technician watching products come off a manufacturing line, but as an artist, a painter, a sculptor, holding a recently completed masterpiece and saying, "Now, that's good!" Which is to say, "It fulfills my creative intention."

God said it is very good, and most of us, most of the time, believe that. Something within the human soul responds instinctively to the goodness, the beauty, the joy of creation. We, too, say with God, "It's good!"

Conversely, when we label a particular action or incident as bad, we are describing what contradicts the harmony, order, and wholeness that these pictures paint of the finished work of creation. This contradiction is described in the second chapter of Genesis in the story theologians have traditionally labeled the Fall, with a capital *F*.

As with the creation narrative, the story of Adam and Eve may suffer from familiarity. We think we know what it says, but it is so encrusted with cultural folk religion that if

CREATION, FALL, AND THEN WHAT?

we actually read it, we might be surprised. It has very little to do with snakes, apples, or missing ribs. The point of this ancient tale of faith is simply this: God loves the creation so much that God gives it freedom. The God who has all authority over creation chooses not to be authoritarian. The God who could control every moment of existence in this planet chooses to saturate the creation with a risky, dangerous freedom. Not only are you and I free, but the created order is free to follow the good purpose of God or to reject it. Even the cells in the body have the freedom to go on a rampage of self-destruction we call cancer. God has neither abandoned the good purpose of the creation nor denied its freedom.

How long has it been since you read "The Adventures of Pinocchio"? Come back with me to Geppetto's toy shop. Picture the old man in your mind, holding his little puppet in his hand. He had imagined it in his dreams, carved it out of wood, shaped it to some extent in his own image. Geppetto loved Pinocchio and would have cared for him; would have ensured that termites never infested his wooden legs; would have kept his strings in order; would have made sure that none of the paint was scraped off Pinocchio's nose. Pinocchio would have been safe and secure. But Pinocchio was not real.

Then the morning came when Geppetto awoke to discover that his wildest dream had come true. His puppet had come to life! But with that life came freedom, and with that freedom all hell broke loose.

Theologians call our abuse of freedom the Fall, and most of us, most of the time, know about that, too. Most of us have experienced it. We know the power of temptation, as subtle as a snake in a fruit tree; the temptation to deny God's good purpose for our lives and go in a selfish direction. We know the shame and guilt that caused Adam and Eve to hide in the bushes rather than stand naked and free before God and each other. We know the conflict between Cain and Abel, the high price of violence, the brutality brought on by jealousy and pride. We have been to the Tower of Babel, unable to understand the people around us.

We know the meaning of the Fall. We know that God's purpose for this world is sometimes thwarted, sometimes abused, sometimes broken, often hidden by the shadows of pain, suffering, conflict, and evil that come as results of that amazing gift of freedom. We believe in the goodness of creation, but we also believe in the Fall.

As we finished a busy summer and looked forward to a frantic autumn, our family took advantage of Labor Day weekend for one more escape to the beach. We spread our toes in the sand, smelled the fresh salt air coming in off the Gulf, and watched the magnificent drama that is performed every evening as the sun sets in the west. We celebrated the goodness of creation and said with God, "This is very good!"

But I had been back in Orlando less than twenty-four hours when I experienced anew the power of the Fall. Six families in our congregation confronted the shocking pain accompanying the discovery of cancer. Two families began the painful process of divorce. We gathered for worship the following Sunday with pictures in our minds of a Pan Am jet held hostage on the tarmac in Pakistan and a terrorist-shattered synagogue in Turkey.

We know about the Fall. We know about the power of evil in the world in which we live. And so, the question becomes, What then? How do we live in a world that does not always fulfill God's good purpose or intention? How do we continue to believe in a good God in an apparently evil world? How do we hold onto our faith in the tension between good and evil? Where in the world is God?

Some scholars date the formulation of the text of Gene-

CREATION, FALL, AND THEN WHAT?

sis in the sixth century B.C., the time of the exile. The violent forces of Babylon had swept across Israel. The people of the covenant had been placed in bondage and were cut off from the land and the community of their faith, isolated from everything that had supported their belief. It appeared that the God of Abraham, Isaac, and Jacob had been defeated by the tyrannical pagan gods of Babylon.

When you read the words of Genesis in that context, you can hear a bold affirmation of faith in the God who brings meaning out of confusion. The creation narrative becomes a shout of defiance from those who, in spite of all evidence to the contrary, continue to trust the God who calls the world into being and declares it "good"; the God who created the astral bodies in the heavens worshiped by their Babylonian captors; the God who has given the creation freedom but has not abandoned a divine, good purpose for it; the God who has not given up on the dream of Eden; the God who is at work to bring the children of Israel home from exile. In the words of Walter Brueggemann in *Genesis:* "This poetry invites the congregation to *confess and celebrate* the world as God has intended it. . . . Giving voice to the poem is itself a line of defense against the press of chaos. It is a way of experiencing the good order of life in the face of disorder."

Hearing the creation narrative recited by despairing exiles gives it the power of men and women who defiantly continue to believe in God when all the circumstances around them contradict their belief; people who continue to proclaim the goodness of God when they find themselves in an evil world. St. Paul reflects this same struggle in his letter to Rome, written to men and women who were experiencing suffering, death, and persecution, readers who could be carried off to the Colosseum at any moment. To them, Paul wrote, "I consider that the sufferings of this present time are not worth comparing with the glory that is to be revealed to us. For the creation waits with eager longing for the revealing of the sons of God. . . . the whole creation has been groaning in travail . . . and not only the creation, but we ourselves, who have the . . . Spirit, groan inwardly as we wait for . . . redemption. . . . If we hope for what we do not see, we wait for it with patience" (Rom. 8:18-25, RSV).

St. Paul expands the struggle of faith into the created order itself. Even nature shares with us the travail of a world that is all too often under the temporary domination of the gods of violence, brutality, suffering, evil, and pain. The earth itself waits for the fulfillment of God's intention, for the goodness of creation to be restored.

St. John, exiled on the island of Patmos, dreamed of the fulfillment of God's creative purpose when he wrote, "I saw a new heaven and a new earth" (Rev. 21:1, RSV). He said that the sea, the Old Testament symbol of chaos, and the physical reality separating John from his people, vanished; it was no more. The Revelation to John is the final version of the restoration of the hope of the creation story, emerging—as did Genesis—out of exile.

There is no escape and there is no easy answer: to live by faith is to live in the constant tension between good and evil, to be caught in the tug and pull of God's good purpose for the creation and the reality of evil around us. But to live by faith is also to know that one day God will see the creation's goodness restored; one day God will see this world again as it was on the first dawn of creation; one day God will say again of the entire created order, "That's very good!"

CHAPTER TWO

The Rainbow Connection

The Christian faith believes that within and beyond the tragedies and the contradictions of history we have laid hold upon a loving heart, the proof of whose love is first impartiality toward all of his children, and secondly a mercy which transcends good and evil.

—Reinhold Niebuhr

READ GENESIS 6–9

It was Sunday morning. The sermon text was the story of Noah and the flood. As I was preparing to leave for the church, my then six-year-old daughter awoke and shouted, "Wow! We really had a flood last night!"

She was correct. The night before, I was putting the finishing touches on the sermon as I sat on the screened porch of our forty-year-old white-frame house and listened to the rumbling roar of the thunder, saw the flash of the lightning, and watched the drenching downpour of rain running off the roof and down the street. I went to sleep with the sound of a soft, steady rain outside the open bedroom windows.

Then Sunday morning came. As the sun began to rise, I was on the porch again. I listened in awe-filled silence as the light began to send a warm glow across the freshly scrubbed trees. The only sound was the occasional chirping of a bird, waking to a new day. In the aftermath of the storm I could almost count the lonely, isolated drops of water still dripping from the roof, the leaves, and the Spanish moss. I could smell the freshness in the air, see the lush color of new grass that would need mowing sooner than I had hoped. Everything around me seemed to be alive, stretching and growing with new life in the beginning of a new day.

Attempting to stretch my senses to take it all in, I cried out, "God! This must be what it was like for Noah on that first morning after the flood, when he opened the door and looked out on a fresh, new world!"

Would that it had actually been that way for Noah! My idyllic image of the morning after was blown away by my friend and Old Testament scholar Dr. Dan G. Johnson, who critiqued this chapter and wrote me this note: "Somehow, I don't think Noah saw anything of the kind after the flood. He must have seen vast devastation with hardly any sign of new life."

I suspect he is correct. The Genesis story is the dramatic portrayal of the disastrous results of human rebellion against God. It begins with individuals—the expulsion of Adam and Eve from the garden, the conflict between Cain and Abel—but it extends to the entire creation.

In his colorful way, Frederick Buechner describes in *Peculiar Treasures* some details of the scene:

> Little by little the waters had risen, first just spreading in over the kitchen linoleum and trickling down the cellar

THE RAINBOW CONNECTION

stairs but eventually floating newspapers and pictures off tables and peeling wallpaper off walls until people were driven to rooftops where they sat wrapped in blankets with their transistor radios on their laps looking up for a break in the clouds and reassuring each other that this must be the clearing shower at last. He remembered the animals he'd had to leave behind—the old sow with her flaxen lashes squealing on top of a hen house as the ripples lapped at her trotters, the elephants awash up to their hips, a marmalade cat with one ragged ear clinging to a TV aerial as a pair of parakeets in a wicker cage floated by over what had once been the elementary school gym.

He also remembered the endless days on the ark—the miserable food, the sea-sickness, the smells. When the downpour finally stopped, he sent birds out to see if they could find any dry land anywhere, and he remembered watching them fly away until they were no bigger than flyspecks on a windowpane, remembered the feeling in his stomach when they finally flew back having found no place to roost.

He remembered especially one of the doves and how, when he saw it returning, he had reached out over the rail, and it had landed on the calluses of his upturned palm. With his eyes closed and tears on his cheeks, he had touched his lips to its feathers, and as he felt the panic of its bird's heart, it had seemed to him that the whole world was just as fragile and as doomed.

For just a moment, put yourself in God's shoes. How would you have felt? What would you have done? You gave life for all creation, shaped and fashioned it after your best design, sustained it with your life-giving presence, and entrusted that creation into the hands of one of those creatures whom you gifted with intelligence and freedom. You intended the whole creation to function in wholeness, harmony, beauty, joy, and peace.

But those free-spirited creatures have become mean-spirited. Created for good, they have turned toward evil. Gifted with freedom, they have acted with utter disregard for the order and purpose you carved into the creation.

How would you feel? What would you have done?

I remember seeing Michelangelo's *Pietà* at the New York World's Fair in 1965. I was moved by the beauty of the work, the perfection with which the sculptor had captured Mary's sorrow as she held the lifeless body of Jesus in her arms. I remember the emotion that welled up within me as I gazed at the masterpiece.

I also remember the emotion I felt on the day a crazed fanatic attacked the *Pietà* with a sledgehammer, breaking off the point of Mary's nose and shattering her delicate marble hand that had reached out in disbelieving grief. But I can only begin to imagine what Michelangelo would have felt if he had seen those shards of his creation on the floor.

I have listened to the cries of frustration and pain from the parents of a rebellious child who, emerging into the tension of adolescence, rejects their values, spurns their love, denies their friendship, and runs headlong down a path toward self-destruction. I have shared the anger of a helpless father who stands in the door and watches his prodigal son head off to some far country (Luke 15).

All of which must be a finite expression of the infinite emotion of God in the story of the flood. The creator described in the Old Testament is not the "unmoved mover" of the universe. This is a passionate God who feels the pain of alienation, who is offended by the evil of the world, and who will ultimately act in judgment against anything that thwarts the divine, good purpose. God's justice is woven so deeply into the fabric of our human existence that we cannot run against the divine goodness without experiencing the divine wrath.

I suspect that if I had been God, I would have been

ready to shut the circus down and start all over. I might have been content to wipe the slate clean, take a few days of vacation, and come back to try it again the next Monday morning. But God's wrath is an expression—not a contradiction—of goodness and grace. Its purpose is redemption, not destruction.

Scanning the horizon of humanity, God found this solitary faithful man; one person who had not sold his soul to the tempter, who had not compromised with evil, who had not surrendered himself to the onslaught of violence, who was "the only good man of his time . . . [and] lived in fellowship with God" (6:10, TEV).

Walter Brueggemann described Noah as "the bearer of an alternative possibility." The solitary presence of Noah affirms that faithfulness and goodness are always possible, even in a world where everything and everyone seem to be driven by evil intent. He was only one man, but he was all God needed to save the world.

It is tempting to turn the spotlight on Noah but, for now, keep the focus on God. The point of the story is not that Noah was good enough to be saved, but that God was able to use this one good man to save the creation. Even as the creation was being destroyed as a result of human sin, God was at work to restore the creation through the faithfulness of this one man.

And God did! God found Noah and warned him of the flood. God was the architect who designed the ark and told Noah how to build it. God was the master veterinarian who gave the instructions for collecting that fantastic floating menagerie. God was the dietitian who made sure they had enough food. God was the weather-forecaster who told them when to get into the ark. And God was the ship's captain who shut the door behind them as the rain began to fall.

The flood came. The earth was destroyed. But Genesis

records, "God had not forgotten Noah and all the animals with him in the boat" (8:1, TEV).

This is not only the God who brings inevitable retribution on everything that contradicts God's good purpose; this is not only the God who finds, calls, and directs Noah; this is also the God who remembers Noah and every part of the creation.

The climax of the drama comes when God gives the command, "Go out of the boat with your wife, your sons, and their wives. Take all the birds and animals out with you, so that they may reproduce and spread over all the earth" (8:16-17, TEV). God makes a covenant with the creation, "never again [to] put the earth under a curse because of what man does" (8:21, TEV). God promises that "as long as the world exists, there will be a time for planting and a time for harvest. There will always be cold and heat, summer and winter, day and night" (8:22, TEV). This is the God who, as a sign of the everlasting covenant, hangs a rainbow in the sky like a string around the divine finger, as a witness to the faithfulness of God.

Now, the important question is, What did this story mean to those early people of the covenant who had been dragged off into exile? How did it encourage and strengthen men and women who had seen everything they valued, everything they loved, everything they trusted, swept away by the forces of Babylon? And how does it speak to us? What effect can this marvelous old tale have on the lives of people like us who face the brutal effects of human suffering and sin?

First, keep the spotlight on God. The flood narrative speaks of the God who takes seriously both the good purpose of the creation and the freedom it has been given. God refuses to abrogate human freedom, even when that

THE RAINBOW CONNECTION

freedom becomes self-destructive. At the same time, God will not abandon the intention of goodness, wholeness, and perfection for the creation.

At least in theory, God could have given the world total freedom, stood back, and let it go spinning on its way to self-destruction. At the opposite extreme, God could have denied the world's freedom, taken absolute control of every inch of existence, and forced the world to fulfill the divine mandate. Either option would have been acceptable for the gods of Babylonia, and both possibilities underlie some common statements I hear today.

I sat on the floor in a circle of youths to talk about God. I knew some of their stories. Several had experienced the pain of having their parents divorce. Two had watched a parent die of cancer. Many had been touched by the recent death of a teenage friend. Most had friends who were using drugs. All of them expressed concern about the possibility of nuclear war. Finally, I asked, "Where is God in all of this? Do you think God is involved in what is going on here?"

One boy immediately responded, "No. God might have gotten the whole thing started, and every now and then he might stick a hand back in to keep things going, but other than that, God just stands off to the side and lets it go."

Another disagreed, "I think God has a purpose for everything. When bad things happen, we may not know why God did it, but someday we will. And in the meantime we just have to believe that God did it for a reason." Near total abandonment or absolute control: which will it be?

The story of Noah offers a shocking alternative. It describes a God who takes seriously both the divine, good purpose for the creation and the freedom it has been given. At the same time, God calls people like Noah into a covenant partnership in fulfilling that purpose.

Now, turn the spotlight on Noah. In the middle of the storm, the flood, the chaos that threatens to overtake the creation, there remains this single witness of faithful living and obedient hope. The Hebrew word for "remnant," which becomes an important concept in the identity and history of the people of Israel, is used for the first time in this narrative. It is to say that God is preserving the creation through this remnant, this small cluster of people and animals in the ark. Through them, the purpose of God is being fulfilled. Through them, the hope for the renewal and restoration of the creation is maintained.

What a word of hope this must have been to the remnant of the people of Israel as they huddled around their campfires in Babylon! They dared to believe that the God who brought Noah through the flood was the same God who would bring them through the exile to the fulfillment of God's promise to them.

Perhaps we need to hear that word, too. In a world fascinated by bigness, power, wealth, and might, it is good to remember that all God needs to fulfill the divine purpose is a remnant of faithful people. Through them, the promise of a renewed creation can be fulfilled.

Bonaro Overstreet wrote one of her best-known poems to "one who doubts the worth of doing anything if you can't do everything":

> You say the little efforts that I make
> will do no good: they never will prevail
> to tip the hovering scale
> where justice hangs in balance
> I don't think
> I ever thought they would.

THE RAINBOW CONNECTION

> But I am prejudiced beyond debate
> in favor of my right to choose which side
> shall feel the stubborn ounces of my weight.

The story of Noah is a story of encouragement for men and women who face the fury of the flood, the crush of chaos, the power of the storm, but who choose to be faithful and who dare to believe that God will be at work through them for the redemption of the world.

Perhaps my idyllic image of the morning after the flood with which I opened this chapter is not all that far from the truth. To live by faith is to look out on a flood-devastated world and believe that by God's re-creative power at work through us, it will once again break forth in new life.

> Great is Thy faithfulness, O God my Father!
> There is no shadow of turning with Thee;
> Thou changest not, Thy compassions, they fail not:
> As Thou hast been Thou forever wilt be.
> Summer and winter, and springtime and harvest,
> Sun, moon and stars in their courses above,
> Join with all nature in manifold witness
> To Thy great faithfulness, mercy and love.

CHAPTER THREE

Acting on the Promises

Faith is not believing without proof, it is trusting without reservation.

—William Sloane Coffin

READ GENESIS 12:1-9, HEBREWS 11:8-16

Recently, prospective students to a major university were asked to submit essays on the question, "If you could spend an evening with any one person, living, deceased, or fictional, whom would you choose and why?" The top three choices of the eight thousand students were God, Jesus, and Lee Iacocca.

Such surveys are always open to change, but if I had the opportunity, I would spend a long evening with Abraham. He is called the "father of the faithful," which is to say that he is the all-time, original prototype of what it means to live by faith, the model of a person who responds in obedience to the spirit of God.

The story of Abraham, indeed, the story of everything we know about the meaning of the word *faith*, begins roughly one thousand seven hundred years before Christ along the riverbank in Haran, where Abraham begins to hear, to feel, to sense, to experience the spirit of God tugging at the coat sleeve of his imagination, saying, "Abraham, get on your feet. Leave your native land, your father's home, and go to a country that I am going to show you." A contemporary version of that call could be, "Come on, Abe! I have better things for you! Get moving!"

One of the most amazing events in the entire drama of human history is that he did it! He packed up his wife Sarah, who was probably starting to wonder if she shouldn't have listened to her mother, and his nephew Lot, who turned out to be more trouble than he was worth, loaded up everything they owned and, like an ancient version of *The Grapes of Wrath*, headed off in the direction of an unknown Promised Land.

The only thing going for them was a promise that went like this: "I will give you many descendants, and they will become a great nation. I will bless you . . . so that you will be a blessing. . . . Through you, I will bless all the nations" (12:2-3, TEV).

Hundreds of years later the writer of the Letter to the Hebrews attempted to define *faith* by saying, "Now faith is the assurance of things hoped for, the conviction of things not seen" (Heb. 11:1, RSV). When he reached for a picture of what that truth looked like, he described Abraham: "By faith Abraham obeyed when he was called to go out to a place which he was to receive as an inheritance. . . . By faith he sojourned in the land of the promise, as in a foreign land. . . . [He] died in faith not having received what was promised, but having seen it from afar" (Heb. 11:8-9, 13, RSV). You cannot read the story of Abraham in the Old Testament, or read the way the New Testament writers retell it, without coming to the conclusion that faith is better understood as a verb than a noun.

Faith is not a noun someone describes from a distance, but a verb we know by experience. To live by faith is to act, to live, to shape our existence on the basis of the promises of God that have yet to be fulfilled; it is to live as if we expect God's intention for wholeness, harmony, peace, freedom, and justice to come true. To live by faith is to be sure of things we hope for; it is to bet our lives on things we cannot yet see.

In the summer of 1986 I flew to Africa to attend a global gathering of Christians. Most of us there experienced some difficulty with jet lag due to the seven-hour time difference between the eastern coast of the United States and the eastern coast of Africa. No one had more difficulty, however, than one of our leaders who arrived just in time for the opening of the conference and did not have the opportunity to adjust to the time change. Unfortunately, he was seated in the center of the platform. During the opening celebration, we watched him hopelessly struggle to keep his eyes open and his head from hitting the table.

It was not his fault that he could not stay awake. His body was still functioning on a different measurement of time, literally, still living in the past. He had not yet begun to live on the basis of the new time.

We faced the same adjustment in learning to think in shillings rather than dollars, with an exchange rate of fifteen to one. One of my most embarrassing moments came after the bellhop delivered my luggage to my room. I reached into my pocketful of Kenyan coins and gave him what I thought was a generous tip, only to discover after he left that I had given him the equivalent of thirty-eight cents. I had not yet begun to think and act on the basis of a new standard of value.

To live by faith is to act on the basis of a new standard of measurement: the new reality of the kingdom, the rule, the will, the way of God revealed in scripture and made plain to us in Jesus Christ. Faith means that we begin to act as if we expect the promises of God to come true, as if God is actually at work in this world.

In the spring of 1986 the bishops of The United Methodist Church issued a pastoral letter on nuclear arms. They pointed out that the letter did not attempt to speak for all nine million United Methodists, nor was it an attempt to force all United Methodists to see the issue from the same point of view. It was, rather, an honest invitation from the spiritual leaders of this church to see this particular issue from the standpoint of faith, to understand the nuclear arms race from the perspective of a biblical understanding of God's intention for creation. It is one attempt to act, to shape our existence, on the basis of the new reality of the kingdom of God rather than to continue living on the old realities of mutually assured destruction. It is a call to live what we believe.

As you read the story of Abraham, you will discover that he attempted to live the life of faith in a very real world, a world chock-full of contradictions and difficulties, an imperfect world filled with imperfect people like us who do not always get the directions clear, who miss turn signals, who are sidetracked along the way. Abraham often finds himself up against hostile powers that threaten to destroy him. He runs head-on into the evil of Sodom and Gomorrah. He gets tangled up in the trickery and deceit of the world around him. Twice he even pretends that Sarah is his sister rather than his wife to try to save his own skin.

If Abraham were living today, he would certainly have a

ACTING ON THE PROMISES

press secretary straighten things out and make him look good. But the point of the story is not that Abraham always did everything right, because he didn't. The point is not that he was always 99.44 percent pure, because he wasn't. The point is not that he ever fully arrived at the promise, because he didn't. The point is that he was faithful along the way. With all his weaknesses, all his confusion, all his stumbling, he was headed in the right direction. To the full extent of his understanding, he acted on the assumption that God's promise would come true.

I have been fascinated with America's fascination with the British royal family. When Harvard celebrated its 350th birthday, the speaker who received the most media attention was Charles, the Prince of Wales. Charles is a man who lives on the basis of a promise. He is not yet the king, and by the appearance of Elizabeth and the longevity of the Queen Mother, it could be a long time until he actually is! But being the Prince of Wales means that he has been given the promise. Until the promise is fulfilled, he lives, talks, walks, dresses, and even plays polo fully expecting to be the king one day. He acts on a promise that has not yet come true.

One of the recent "Abrahams" in my life was Harold Francis. Retired from Goodwill Industries when he moved to Florida, he had been around preachers and churches for a long time and knew the good and the bad, the "ins" and the "outs" of preachers and congregations. He was a loyal layperson who loved his church enough to be honest with his pastor and who could be trusted to protect a confidence, do a job, and keep me humble. Hardly a day went by that he did not stop by the office to see if there was something he could do.

Harold was not perfect. In fact, he could be downright cantankerous. He figured he had reached the age where he did not need to try to please everyone anymore. But he loved life, he loved his church, and it was because of his outstretched hand and warm friendship that a large number of people half his age were drawn into our fellowship.

Harold had experienced three heart attacks in ten years. He knew the risk when the cardiologist told him he needed surgery. With surgery, there was a fifty-fifty chance that he could die on the table; without it, he would be forced to live as a semi-invalid, waiting for the "big bullet" to hit.

He chose surgery. When I visited him the night before the operation, he gave me some notes he had been writing while he was in the hospital:

> Five minutes after my surgeon told me this, I burst into tears—of *all* the people, *me* crying like a 5 year old—my nurse came in, asked if I was afraid—me? Well, maybe, but most of all my thoughts were for my loved ones—after all, Lois and I have been married 45 years in June—but more than my family I could think of hundreds of friends I love so much.
>
> Since Feb. 7, 1975, I have had three attacks—one of my doctors said I had missed the big bullet by inches because we were able to get prompt attention, but this couldn't continue—he also said he didn't think God was finished with me yet! At my age, etc. what would God have me do!
>
> It is now 8:00 P.M.—It's been a long day—I do have a good feeling about the outcome of the surgery, however which way it turns out—life or death, I know of the many prayers said for me, and also the love of each other.
>
> What I now have is the words to an old hymn—"Standing on the Promises of God!" I do believe and I do love you all.

Harold died on the operating table. His heart, which had given so much to others, could give no more. When the church family he had helped form gathered for worship in his memory, we sang his hymn:

> Standing on the promises of Christ my King,
> Through eternal ages let his praises ring;
> Glory in the highest, I will shout and sing,
> Standing on the promises of God.
>
> Standing on the promises that cannot fail,
> When the howling storms of doubt and fear assail,
> By the living Word of God I shall prevail,
> Standing on the promises of God.
>
> Standing on the promises of Christ the Lord,
> Bound to him eternally by love's strong cord,
> Overcoming daily with the Spirit's sword,
> Standing on the promises of God.
>
> Standing on the promises I cannot fall,
> Listening every moment to the Spirit's call,
> Resting in my Savior as my all-in-all,
> Standing on the promises of God.

To live by faith, to follow the model of Abraham, is to hear God calling us to a new way of life and to begin living and acting on the confident assurance that God's promise will be fulfilled.

CHAPTER FOUR

Strangely Blessed

I have the feeling the Lord has laid his hands on you, and that is a dangerous, dangerous thing.

—Bayard Rustin to Martin Luther King, Jr.

READ GENESIS 12–15, HEBREWS 11:32-40

God said, "I will bless you and through you all the nations of the world shall be blessed." And it might not have sounded like such an outrageous figment of divine imagination if God had been talking to anyone but Abraham. If God had spoken those words to someone with power, someone with authority, someone with some genuine, honest-to-goodness clout; if the promise had been given to someone with money and prestige; if God had spoken to the president of the United States, the CEO of a multinational corporation, or the general secretary of the U.N.; if the word had come to a TV personality, a world-famous athlete, or even a television evangelist; if God had said this to anyone but Abraham, it might have made sense. But God chose a nondescript, desert nomad with very little going for him and said, "I will bless you and through you all the nations of the world shall be blessed."

Theologians call that act of God "election." When you look at the story of Abraham, you begin to suspect that "election" means that the very guy who could not have gotten himself elected to clean up after the camels is exactly the one God votes in as the "chosen one," chosen not for privilege or or comfort, but for the terrifying responsibility of being the one through whom God will bless the world.

The descendants of Abraham, and we with them, have had a difficult time living with that promise. They liked the part where God said, "I will bless you." Throughout scripture are fragments of the hope that being blessed by God will mean immunity from pain and suffering or protection from danger and risk. Perhaps being blessed means that we will get all the "goodies" and come off better than anybody else.

But what Abraham discovered, what the prophets declared, what Jesus knew, and what you and I continuously need to learn is that being blessed by God means being called to be a blessing to others. We are not saved from the world for ourselves, but by God's grace we are saved from ourselves for the sake of the world. We are chosen not for privilege but for service. We are chosen to share in the suffering of a broken world. We are chosen to be part of the healing of the pain of the world. To be blessed by God means we are called, chosen, claimed as men and women through whom God will bless the world, and that is a very costly and a very dangerous business.

Many of us grew up saying a bedtime prayer that went something like this: "God bless Mama, God bless Daddy, God bless Grandma, God bless my dog Spot, and God bless Roger the gerbil." If we ran out of names, we might say, "And God bless everyone in the world." It was a well-intentioned prayer, but biblically it won't wash. The unsettling fact of biblical faith is that God does not generally bless the world en masse. God chooses to bless the world through particular people in particular places at particular times, people who make themselves available, at great cost to themselves, to become the channels through which God's love, goodness, justice, and peace are revealed to a dark and dangerous world. To be blessed by God means we are called to be among the people whom God will use as a blessing, people who make God's presence known in the world.

The writer of the Letter to the Hebrews gives this all-too-vivid description of what it looks like to be a part of that company of "blessed" people: "Others, refusing to accept freedom, died under torture in order to be raised to a better life. Some were mocked and whipped, and others were put in chains and taken off to prison. They were stoned, they were sawn in two, they were killed by the sword. They went around clothed in skins of sheep or goats—poor, persecuted, and mistreated. The world was not good enough for them" (Heb. 11:35-38, TEV). Hold that picture up against some of the popular forms of you-can-have-it-all religion sweeping the country today, and you will realize just how strange the blessing of God can be.

I have been filling a now bulging file folder with the stories of contemporary saints who are living out that strange blessing today. Although the cynics are suggesting that there are really no heroes anymore, only celebrities, these persons are heroes for me. They are among those persons who have been blessed by God so that they can be a blessing to the world. Let me share a few of their stories with you.

I know of a Methodist pastor in a territory controlled by the Soviet Union. This territory was independent until it was taken over by the Soviet Union. It has a long history, a strong culture, a deep sense of its own identity. Across the past two generations, the people there have faced a massive immigration of Russians and the fear that they will lose their cultural, historical, and religious identity. The resentments run deep. One of the things that the pastor did may not sound very significant until you see it in that setting. The Methodist church he serves started holding Russian language services. When a friend in the United States asked why, the pastor said, "I can carry no bitterness toward these people. Somehow I must find a way to share the gospel with them and make them my brothers and sisters in Jesus Christ."

One of this man's dreams was to come to the United States and study at Asbury Theological Seminary. Every time he tried, however, the government refused to give him permission. Then one summer day, a friend of mine received a surprising phone call. It was the pastor. He was at Lake Junaluska, North Carolina. He visited the seminary and spoke in the chapel. He said, "The fact that I stand before you today is a miracle." My friend said, "I believe it's a miracle, too."

But the story does not begin or end with this man. He grew up in the same congregation under the influence of a previous pastor, who was there when Stalin came to power. The authorities told the pastor to close the church. He said no. He was tried and sentenced to twenty years in a labor camp. He spent four years there until Stalin died. When he was released, he raised up the current pastor. He, too, said, "I hold no bitterness against them!" Like Alexander Solzhenitsyn, he said that his time in that labor camp was a time to draw close to God.

The world is not good enough for people like this. I want to break bread with this pastor and lift a glass to his mentor. I want to claim them as persons whom God has strangely blessed and through whom God is blessing all the nations of the world.

The strife-torn nation of South Africa is producing more than its share of strangely blessed saints. The world is familiar with the name and smile of Archbishop Desmond Tutu. Not so familiar is the name of Ndanganeni Phaswana, a thirty-six-year-old South African Lutheran pastor who spent a year at St. Olaf College in Minnesota. Precisely because he is unknown, he represents the host of nameless saints who remain faithful to the call of God in spite of overwhelming oppression.

During his imprisonment in his home country, he was tortured with electric shock through electrodes attached to his body. For hours on end, he was subjected to this treatment. The shocks were so intense that he involuntarily bit his lips and tongue until they were bloody. This torture went on for six days. In solitary confinement, he prayed, "Okay, if you do exist, allow me to experience what Christ experienced on Calvary." He took the posture of crucifixion and had a vision of Christ, who "showed me his scars, and they were just like mine."

The pastor had no way of knowing that people outside were working constantly for his release. Suddenly, without official explanation, the charges were dropped and he was released. He was brought to St. Olaf to rest and recuperate. The students and faculty were left in awe and would have been happy for him to stay longer, but he chose to go back to his homeland, not unlike Dietrich Bonhoeffer who chose to leave the United States and go back to Nazi Germany just prior to World War II. Phaswana said, "I feel obliged to go back and serve my people the gospel. Anybody who preaches against apartheid, who preaches the gospel, is in danger. But I'm still preaching the gospel, and I'll do it until the day I die."

I would like to break bread with Phaswana and lift a cup

to the brothers and sisters who are strangely blessed in South Africa as they continue to work for justice, harmony, and peace. Through them, God is blessing the people of the world.

There is, of course, a danger in telling stories like these. The subtle danger is that we will begin to think that the life of faith is only for persons with dramatic and powerful stories to tell. But there was nothing heroic, nothing memorable, nothing famous about Abraham. He was an ordinary nomad when God blessed him so that he would be a blessing to the world. The blessing of God is given to ordinary saints, men and women who make themselves available to God and are willing to be the agents of God's blessing wherever they find themselves.

I talked with a young woman who, in her first appointment out of seminary, was sent to a dying church. She found the people discouraged and demoralized. But with a profound sense of God's calling in her life and an elflike smile on her face, she said, "We are so desperate that we will welcome just about anyone into our church, and that's grace." Responding to her faith, the people of the congregation have begun to dream of a new future. They are reaching out to the "just about anyones" around them. The members sense that the church's life is not over, that God has new work for them to do. They have been blessed with a new sense of God's calling to be a blessing to their community.

It can happen. Just as it happened for Abraham, it can happen for us. We can be the persons through whom this world will be strangely blessed.

CHAPTER FIVE

Learning to Laugh with God

Humor belongs to the faithful, . . . because they know that whatever happens is not the last word. . . . At the end is God and even now, within this experience, God is with us.

—Gene Zimmerman

READ GENESIS 18:1-15, 21:1-8

In *A Book of Travellers' Tales*, Eric Newby collected the stories of three hundred wanderers, spanning two thousand four hundred years, covering virtually the entire earth. From a Greek navigator who landed on the British Isles around 310 B.C. to travelers in the nineteenth and twentieth centuries, he tells the often humorous, sometimes frustrating stories of their discoveries and disappointments. In his review of the book, Paul Gray came to the conclusion that "the perennial appeal of the open road is the possibility of surprise."

No travelers of the open road were ever more surprised than Abraham and Sarah when they discovered God's promise was going to come true, a baby was on the way. In his irrepressible style, Frederick Buechner describes Sarah as an old woman who, after a lifetime in the desert, has a face that is "cracked and rutted like a six-month drought." He helps us see her as she hunches her shoulders around her ears and her body begins to shake: "She squints her eyes shut, and her laughter is all china teeth and wheeze and tears running down as she rocks back and forth in her kitchen chair." She is laughing at the surprise of a ninety-one-year-old woman having a baby. Abraham tries to keep a straight face, but he finally gives in to the outrageous surprise of it all and starts laughing, too. Then Buechner discusses the cause of their laughter:

> The old woman's name is Sarah, of course, and the old man's name is Abraham, and they are laughing at the idea of a baby's being born in the geriatric ward and Medicare's picking up the tab. They are laughing because the angel not only seems to believe it but seems to expect them to believe it too. They are laughing because with part of themselves they do believe it. They are laughing because with another part of themselves they know it would take a fool to believe it. They are laughing because laughing is better than crying and maybe not even all that different. They are laughing because if by some crazy chance it should just happen to come true, then they would really have something to laugh about.

The story of the fulfillment of God's promise begins with an old woman laughing. And perhaps if we are to walk the road of faith, we need to listen for that laughter, too. Before it is anything else, it is the laughter of disbelief. If you could translate it into words, it would say, "God, you have got to be kidding!" It is the laughter of doubt, wondering if God can really pull off what has been promised.

LEARNING TO LAUGH WITH GOD

There is good reason for Sarah to laugh the laughter of disbelief. The whole story is based on the premise that she is barren, childless, which in the Old Testament is a word picture of what it means to be a people with no future, a people who have no hope and no human way of creating it. Little wonder that when the angel tells Sarah to start cleaning up the nursery, order the diaper service, and schedule the Lamaze classes, she laughs out loud and asks, "Now that I am old and worn out, can I still enjoy sex? And besides, my husband is old too" (18:12, TEV).

The people of Israel must have laughed the laughter of disbelief when, hapless and desolate in exile, the prophet promised that one day they would return to Jerusalem. The hope of return must have been as difficult to believe as the promise of a child for Abraham and Sarah. They laughed, and if we are honest with ourselves, we laugh that way sometimes, too.

We try to deny it. We try to stifle it the way Sarah did—hold it inside, turn it into a cough like teenagers do when they giggle in church on Sunday morning. We try to deny the laughter, particularly when we come to church, particularly when we hang around with religious folks. In fact, some religious groups will tell you that if you have any disbelief, any doubt, any questions, if you are not certain of everything, you are not going to make it. That kind of religion says, "God promised it; I believe it; that settles it." That didn't settle it for Abraham and Sarah. That didn't settle it for anyone I can find in the Old Testament. That didn't settle it for Jesus. Read again the story of his prayer in the Garden of Gethsemane (Matt. 26:36-43). That probably won't settle it for most of us.

It is not always easy to believe that God's promise will be fulfilled in our lives. It is one thing to hear God promise Abraham that he will have descendants as numerous as the stars in the sky, but when it comes down to it, something in us wants to say, "God, you've got to be kidding! Not actually in our lifetimes, not in our experience!" We have a tendency to believe that all our possibilities have been exhausted, there is no future for us, no new hope or new direction. And so we laugh the laughter of disbelief.

You can hear that kind of laughter throughout the Gospels if you listen for it. You can hear it on the hillside the day Jesus looked at the crowds, turned to the disciples, and said, "Fellows, these folks are hungry. You give them something to eat." The disciples answered, "Lord, you've got to be kidding! All we have are five loaves and two fishes. How can we feed a crowd like this?" (Matt. 14:16-17).

You can hear that laughter the day Jesus stood beside the tomb of his friend, Lazarus, and said, "Show me where you laid him." Lazarus's sister responded in surprise, "Jesus, there is going to be a great stench if we open the grave. He has been dead for four days!" (John 11:39). They were crying, but beneath their tears they were laughing: "Lord, you've got to be kidding! There is nothing you can do in this situation. The story is over, finished. There are no new possibilities."

You can hear that kind of laughter the day they marched Jesus through the city to the hill where they nailed him to the cross. The Gospel writers record that the crowd mocked him, saying, "He wanted to save others; he can't even save himself!" (Matt. 27:42; Mark 15:31; Luke 23:35-36).

You can hear that kind of laughter from some of his most faithful disciples on the morning of the resurrection. When the women came running back with the report that they had discovered the empty tomb, these first disciples who would become the apostles, the saints of the early church, called their reports nonsense, the chatter of foolish women.

I suspect that if we are honest enough to name the sounds deep inside our own souls, we know that laughter, too. Perhaps the journey of faith will begin for us in that place where we, with Sarah, are willing to name that laughter and admit that we do not quite believe the promise of God.

Listen for it in the world, listen in your own soul, and keep listening for eight or nine months. Then you will hear laughing again. This time it is a different kind of laughter altogether. This time it is laughter that comes up from the same place as tears. It is the laughter that bursts from a woman's soul when she hears her cries mingled with the cries of a newborn child. It is the laughter of labor pain transformed into a new birth. It is the kind of laughter that breaks out when we least expect it from the depths of sorrow, barrenness, loneliness, hopelessness, or tears.

The writer of Genesis says, "The Lord blessed Sarah, as he had promised, and she became pregnant and bore a son to Abraham when he was old. The boy was born at the time God had said he would be born" (21:1-2, TEV).

What they had always hoped for but never dared to expect happened! These two old coots, who had absolutely no human reason to expect that the promise would be fulfilled, were surprised by the gift of God's goodness and grace. When it happened, Sarah announced, "God has brought me joy and laughter. Everyone who hears about it will laugh with me" (21:6, TEV). The final touch was their naming the child Isaac, meaning "God laughs," which is at least to say that God was in on the surprise and laughed the whole way to the delivery room.

If you listen, you can hear that kind of laughter throughout the Old Testament. It is the laughter of the surprising, unexpected goodness and grace of God. You can hear it at Bethel when Jacob awakes out of his troubled sleep to shout, "The Lord is here! He is in this place and I didn't know it!" (28:16, TEV).

You can hear it on the day that Jacob, expecting to face the wrath of his brother Esau, is accepted with open arms. As they cry for joy on each other's shoulders, Jacob rejoices, "To see your face is for me like seeing the face of God, now that you have been so friendly to me" (33:10, TEV).

You can hear that laughter of surprising grace in the amazement of the children of Israel as they, expecting to be destroyed by the Egyptians, sink their feet into the wet clay of the divided Red Sea and march off to freedom (Exod. 14).

You can hear it in the wonder of the exiles when they heard the Lord say,

> For a long time I kept silent. . . .
> But now the time to act has come;
>   I cry out like a woman in labor. . . .
> I will lead my blind people by roads they
>   have never traveled.
> I will turn their darkness into light
>   and make rough country smooth before them.
> —Isaiah 42:14-16, TEV

> Go out from Babylon, go free!
> Shout the news gladly; make it known everywhere:
> "The Lord has saved his servant Israel!"
> —Isaiah 48:20, TEV

> You will leave Babylon with joy;
>   you will be led out of the city in peace.
> The mountains and hills will burst into singing,
>   and the trees will shout for joy.
> —Isaiah 55:12, TEV

You can hear that laughter throughout the gospel. It is the

laughter of the surprising gift of God's grace when we least expect or deserve it.

Listen for it on the lips of a young woman named Mary in Luke's Gospel. In many ways she is a parallel to Sarah. The angel comes to her and tells her she is going to have a child. Mary asks, "How can this be since I am still a virgin?" The angel says there is nothing that is impossible with God, which is the answer to the question the angel asked Abraham and Sarah, "Is there anything too difficult for God?" Mary replies, "Let it be to me as you say," and she finally bursts into singing, "My soul rejoices in God my savior, it magnifies the Lord, who has seen fit to bless his handmaiden" (Luke 1:34, 38, 46-48).

It is the laughter of a lame man who walks back home, a blind man who can see, a leper who is restored to health, all because they met this stranger from Nazareth along the road one day.

It is the laughter that bubbles beneath the parables of Jesus when he promises that one day street people and bag ladies are going to be invited into the bridal feast. One day the housekeeper will find her lost coin, the shepherd will find his lost sheep, and someday the loving father will laugh uproariously because his wandering son has found his way home.

It is the laughter of St. John in the Revelation, when he describes the great throng of saints gathered around the throne who hear a voice saying, "I'll make all things new. I'll be their God, and they'll be my people. There will be no more tears, crying, sorrow, or pain, for the old things have passed away and I have made everything new" (Rev. 21:1-5).

It is the laughter that wells up in our souls when we suddenly discover that we are loved not because we ever earned or deserved it, but simply because we are children of God. It is the laughter that breaks through our despair when we realize there are new possibilities, new hopes, new directions, new challenges for us; our story is not yet over. Whatever has gone before, God has some new opportunity for us in the future. It is the laughter that is the only honest human response to the surprising, outrageous, unexpected gift of God's goodness and grace.

We had a visitor in our church family last summer from the little town of Olney, England, whose only claim to fame is that it was the hometown of two famous poets in the eighteenth century. One was John Newton. He grew up in what we would call an abusive home. His mother died when he was very young. His father was a brutal sea captain. Newton became a fugitive from the law and ran a slave ship between England and Africa. But along the way he was surprised by the discovery of the love of God in Jesus Christ. His life was transformed. He became a priest serving the Anglican church in Olney. It was Newton who wrote,

> Amazing grace! how sweet the sound
> That saved a wretch like me!
> I once was lost, but now am found,
> Was blind but now I see.

The other poet was William Cowper. In many ways his story was even more tragic than Newton's. From a very early age he was afflicted by severe fits of depression. He tried to commit suicide several times and spent some time in an asylum. He was released from the asylum and a short while later was taken to Olney where he lived next door to the village vicar, John Newton, who befriended him. It was probably Newton's friendship that saved Cowper's life and sanity. Newton taught him to garden and to work with wood. They worshiped together in the village church, and they wrote poetry. They combined about three hundred

LEARNING TO LAUGH WITH GOD

hymns into a book published as *The Olney Hymns,* which became a classic of British poetry in the late eighteenth century.

The joy and peace were not to last. Cowper's depression returned. The darkness closed in. He suffered from horrible nightmares and uncontrollable anxiety. Newton saw him through the darkness until he came into the light once more. He then lived in relatively normal health for another twenty years, when madness returned.

It was out of his experience of depression and hope, that combination of darkness and light, that Cowper wrote his part of the Olney hymns, one of which affirms his faith in the God who surprises the people of faith:

> Sometimes a light surprises
> The Christian while he sings;
> It is the Lord, who rises
> With healing in his wings.
> When comforts are declining,
> He grants the soul again
> A season of clear shining,
> To cheer it after rain.
> Though vine nor fig tree neither
> Their wonted fruit should bear,
> Though all the field should wither,
> Nor flocks nor herds be there;
> Yet God the same abiding,
> His praise shall tune my voice,
> For while in him confiding,
> I cannot but rejoice.

Listen closely. Listen to the world in which you live. Listen to the words of scripture. But most of all, listen closely to your own soul and perhaps you will hear the laughter of disbelief. But if you wait in faith, you will also hear the laughter that is the only appropriate response to the surprising grace and goodness of God. Keep the ears of your soul alert and perhaps you will discover the possibility of surprise that is the perennial appeal of the open road of faith.

Sarah said, "God has brought me joy and laughter. Everyone who hears about it will laugh with me" (21:6, TEV).

CHAPTER SIX

The Road to Mount Moriah

The hardness of God is kinder than the softness of men, and his compulsion is our liberation.

—C. S. Lewis

READ GENESIS 22:1-19, HEBREWS 11:17-19

"It was faith that made Abraham offer his son Isaac . . . when God put Abraham to the test" (Heb. 11:17, TEV). There you have the condensed version of one of the most soul-stirring stories recorded in the Old Testament. It is the shorthand account of a trip to one of the highest spiritual mountaintops in the history of faith. It is the abridged edition of one of the most perfectly told short stories anywhere in literature. This story has obviously been told and retold so many times, by so many storytellers of the faith, that it has been honed of every wasted word, trimmed to perfection. It is like a priceless diamond that has been polished so that it reflects the truth almost too clearly for us to receive it.

The story begins like this: "Some time later God tested

Abraham; he called to him, 'Abraham!' And Abraham answered, 'Yes, here I am!' 'Take your son,' God said, 'your only son, Isaac, whom you love so much, and go to the land of Moriah. There on a mountain that I will show you, offer him as a sacrifice to me' " (22:1-2, TEV).

I cannot read that last sentence without feeling chills running up and down my spine. Even accounting for the fact that this story comes out of a culture and time in which child sacrifice was commonplace, God's demand drops as a massive depth charge into the middle of the story of Abraham, vibrating everything around it.

Isaac was much more than Abraham's son, although God knows that would have been enough. Isaac was Abraham's only hope of ever seeing God's purpose fulfilled. Isaac was the one and only chance for Abraham to have descendants as countless as the stars in the sky, as numberless as the sand on the shore in accordance with God's covenant. Isaac was the only hope Abraham had, and now the God who had started the whole thing by calling Abraham to go to a land God would show him places this shocking requirement before him: "Take your son, your only son, Isaac whom you love so much, to Mount Moriah and offer him as a sacrifice."

From the opening sentence, we know that this story will lead us away from the cheap, shallow religion that passes for faith in our society and will hurl us out into the costly depths of faith, depths into which most of us are very hesitant to plunge.

I think if I had been Abraham I would have slept in the next morning. I would have taken my time, stalled, put the thing off awhile. Abraham evidently understood that there are some things in life that, if put off, may never be done at all. So early the next morning we see the old man cutting his wood for the sacrifice, loading up his donkey, calling two of his most trusted servants, gathering up his son Isaac, and starting off for the land of Moriah, for the mountain the Lord had shown him.

I find this a fascinating sentence: "On the third day Abraham saw the place in the distance" (22:4, TEV). On the third day—there was no way that the storytellers of Genesis in their wildest dreams could have imagined what that phrase would mean for people of faith on this side of the resurrection, Christians who affirm the words of the Nicene Creed that Christ "rose again on the third day according to the Scriptures." Abraham never could have imagined that. Perhaps the spirit of God could! But we must stay with Abraham on the third day when he "saw the place in the distance. Then he said to the servants, 'Stay here with the donkey. The boy and I will go over there and worship, and then we will come back to you.' Abraham made Isaac carry the wood for the sacrifice, and he himself carried a knife and live coals for starting the fire" (22:4-6, TEV). There is not a detail missing here. Abraham is not going to get up on the mountain and say, "Oops, I forgot my lighter!" He even has live coals; every detail is included.

"As they walked along together" (22:6, TEV)—I want you to hold that picture of Abraham and his son, the son he loved so much, walking along together. "Isaac spoke up, 'Father!' He answered, 'Yes, my son?' Isaac asked, 'I see that you have the coals and the wood, but where is the lamb for the sacrifice?' " (22:7, TEV). How would you like to have tried to answer that question? Abraham's response is either a bold-faced lie or one of the most profound statements of faith recorded anywhere in scripture. Abraham answered, "God himself will provide one" (22:8, TEV).

By faith, Abraham is choosing to trust in the goodness of God, even when the circumstances around him seem to contradict it. He will continue to believe that somehow God will provide a way for God's good purpose to be fulfilled, even when everything seems to work against it. The Lord will provide.

You can find this quality of faith in other characters in the Bible. Do you remember the story of Job? We find Job, having lost his wealth, his lands, and most of his heirs, sitting on the ash heap of his fondest hopes and highest dreams, scratching the boils on his behind with a piece of broken pottery. His not-too-encouraging wife says, "Why don't you curse God and die?" (Job 2:9, TEV). How would you like to get that kind of encouragement from your spouse? Through his suffering, Job continues to say, "Though he slay me, yet I will trust him" (Job, 15:15, KJV). There is a depth of faith I don't think I have begun to plunge. Out of that same depth of faith Abraham responds to the question of his son, "The Lord will provide."

From here, the story is like a movie from Steven Spielberg; it is *Indiana Jones* all over again, filled with split-second timing, as the narration builds toward the surprise twist in the drama. We watch in amazement as Abraham arranges the wood on the altar. We gasp in disbelief as he ties the boy's hands and feet and lifts his adolescent body onto the wood. Then, hardly willing to watch but unable to tear our eyes away, we see the old man take the knife, lift it up into the air, and prepare to send it plunging into his son's body. But, in that micro-second between the raising of the knife and the movement of the muscles that would have ended Isaac's life, a voice comes from somewhere in the clouds. Abraham recognizes it as the angel of the Lord, calling him just as he had been called before, "Abraham! Abraham!" Almost disbelieving the gracious interruption of his awesome task, Abraham shouts back, "Yes, here I am!" The angel commands him, "Do not hurt the boy or do anything to him . . . Now I know that you have obedient reverence for God, because you have not kept back your only son from him" (22:12).

THE ROAD TO MOUNT MORIAH

The conclusion to the story comes almost as a postscript:

> The angel of the Lord called to Abraham from heaven a second time, "I make a vow by my own name—the Lord is speaking—that I will richly bless you. Because you did this and did not keep back your only son from me, I promise that I will give you as many descendants as there are stars in the sky or grains of sand along the seashore. Your descendants will conquer their enemies. All nations will ask me to bless them as I have blessed your descendants—all because you obeyed my command." Abraham went back to his servants, and they went together to Beersheba, where Abraham settled.
> —22:15-19, TEV

The final scene is the reaffirmation of the covenant that began the entire drama, the reaffirmation of the great promise God gave to Abraham.

What will you do with a story like that? Most of us do an effective job avoiding it! I thumbed through books of collected sermons, and in a quick survey of the preachers whose sermons are included there, I could not find one who had the nerve to preach on this story. It is a story we would like to avoid. But it is in scripture, and if we think about it, it is here in your life and mine as well.

The point of the story may be that while grace is free, maturity in the faith is very costly. Although God's love is simple, living it is never easy. Although the journey of faith is full of joyful surprise, the kind of laughter to which Isaac's name bears witness, it is also filled with sacrifice. Sooner or later, men and women who choose to walk the road of faith will be led toward Moriah, to the place where they are called to offer to God the one and only thing they may be tempted to love more than they love God.

As I wrestled with this story, I caught, in the corner of

my imagination, the picture of the New Testament character we call the "rich young ruler" (Matt. 19:16-24; Mark 10:17-25; Luke 18:18-25). The title alone means he had everything going for him. You can see him rolling up to Jesus in his brightly polished red Porsche, designer labels on all his clothes, his hair groomed just right, exactly the right tone in his tan. But his life has become dry and stale, with all the zing of a wet tennis ball. He comes to Jesus in much the same way many of us come to worship: "Master, tell me what I have to do to inherit eternal life." What must I do to catch hold of the kind of life I see in you? How can I wrap my hand around life that is really alive, vibrant, worth living? What must I do to gain life?

The Gospel writers say that Jesus looked at him and loved him. Jesus asked, "How are you doing on the Ten Commandments?" The young man replied, "Oh, I have kept all those from my youth up. I have all my Sunday school pins here; I sang in the youth choir and went to my youth group every Sunday night. Then I went away to college, got out of the habit, and have not been very religious since. I've bent a few of the commandments, but I haven't really broken any of them. I think I'm doing pretty well."

Here the Gospel writers say that Jesus looked at him again, looked at him so deeply that the Master could see exactly what motivated him, the thing that had control of this young man's life. Jesus said, "There is only one thing you lack. There is only one thing standing between you and the life God has called you to live. Only one thing is keeping you from discovering the new future God has for you. Go, sell everything you have and give it to the poor, and then follow me."

You could have knocked that young man over with the fizz of his soft drink. The Gospel writers say he went away sorrowfully because he had great riches. I have often wondered if the problem was that he had great riches or that the great riches had him. The things he possessed had taken possession of him. His wealth, his possessions, his pride, his prestige, had control over his life and held him in such bondage that he was no longer free to rise up and move into the life he knew he wanted to live. His attitude toward his wealth kept him a prisoner and would not allow him to discover what it means to be blessed and be a blessing to the whole world.

Abraham was called to offer his son, his only son, the son he loved so much. For the rich young ruler, it was his possessions, his attitude toward his wealth. I wonder what it is for you and for me? I wonder what stands between us and the call of God in our lives? I wonder what one thing we would be tempted to love more than we love God? I wonder what it is in your life and mine to which the spirit of God would point and say, "Take that thing you love and go to the mountain and offer it to me"?

The phone was ringing as I unlocked the office door one Monday morning. I could hear the urgency in the woman's voice as she asked if she could stop in on her way to work. She said she had something she needed to do and wanted me to pray with her about it. In ten minutes she was in my office. In five minutes she poured out her story. She had fallen in love with a married man. They had kept in touch by mail after he moved to a distant city. A year ago she returned to the church, hoping to rebuild the moral integrity of her life. It worked. She said she began to feel a sense of "rightness" in her life. Now the time had come for a painfully difficult act of faith.

She had written a letter to her friend, telling him she had to break off the relationship It did not *feel* good, but she knew it *was* good. She was ready to put the letter in the mail and wanted me to pray with her for the strength to do what she knew was right. With tears, we prayed together. There was no way to remove the pain, the tremendous emotional cost of her action, but the Lord provided the strength for her to do what she knew she needed to do.

I saw her some time later. She said that the memory of the relationship still hurt, but she had found new freedom, a new sense of wholeness in her relationship with God, and a new sense of self-esteem. She had been to Mount Moriah, and she knew that the Lord provides.

The son of an outstanding pastor had wrestled with his identity as "the preacher's son" and with the meaning of the word *success*. He wrote me a letter describing his experience:

> A lot has happened since I wrote last. Over Thanksgiving I read *The Becomers* [by Keith Miller]. His understanding of Christian growth was refreshing—and disturbing. It made me search my heart about an unsurrendered area of my life. I guess being my father's son has had something to do with it. I think I've always felt like I've had to measure up to him in the ministry and so, all through seminary, the fear of failure, of being a nobody in some little country church, bothered me a lot. But always in the back of my mind I had a way out. . . . I would get a Ph.D. That would somehow insure my success. As I read Miller I saw myself hanging on that trapeze bar that had "success" and "Ph.D." written all over it and God was pushing another one toward me that simply said, "Be a minister and let me have your future regardless of whether it means success or failure." As I was driving home from Ohio after Thanksgiving, I finally let go. It was very unemotional and even uncertain but in the days to come a deep inner contentment came over me.

He had been to Mount Moriah, to the place in his own soul where he was called to surrender to God the one

THE ROAD TO MOUNT MORIAH

thing that had a fighting chance of standing in the way of God's purpose for his life, and he discovered that the Lord provides.

C. S. Lewis's journey to Mount Moriah occurred while he was riding up Headington Hill on the top of a bus. He described the way God offered "what now appears to be a wholly free choice. . . . Without words and (I think) almost without images, a fact about myself was somehow presented to me." In language that Abraham would have understood, Lewis wrote,

> Not the slightest assurance . . . was offered to me. Total surrender, the absolute leap in the dark, were demanded. The reality with which no treaty can be made was upon me. . . . The demand was simply "All." . . . I became aware that I was holding something at bay, or shutting something out. Or, if you like, that I was wearing some stiff clothing, like corsets, or even a suit of armor. . . . I felt myself being, there and then, given a free choice. I could open the door or keep it shut; I could unbuckle the armor or keep it on. . . . I knew that to open the door or to take off the corset meant the incalculable.

Lewis described his moment of surrender by simply saying, "I unbuckled my armor and the snowman started to melt."

On the top of a bus, riding up Headington Hill, C. S. Lewis experienced what Abraham learned on the way up Mount Moriah: "On the mountain, the Lord provides."

I cannot promise where it will happen or how the call will come to you. I can promise only that if you choose to follow the road of faith, sooner or later it will lead to your own Mount Moriah—the place where you surrender to God the greatest love of your life, and the place where you discover that the Lord provides.

CHAPTER SEVEN

If You Don't Do It . . .

> There's a divinity that shapes our ends,
> Rough-hew them how we will.
> —William Shakespeare

READ GENESIS 25:19-34, 27:1-29, 28:10-22

No single fact is more basic to the story of my life than this: I have a twin brother. I cannot define my identity without including my womb-mate who arrived in this world four minutes after me and has been tied to my identity ever since. We grew up in the same community, attended the same schools, graduated from the same college and seminary. Our paths separated when Jack followed his wife back to Michigan and I followed mine to Florida.

In spite of our obvious similarities, our relationship was not always idyllic. We were what child psychologists call "strong-willed children," who sometimes shared all the intimacy of two cats in a burlap bag. The evidence of our struggle of wills was left on the bottom panels of the bedroom doors in the house on Grand Avenue, most of which were scarred when one brother chased the other into the room and then stood outside kicking the door while the offended twin locked himself inside. Imbedded in the family history is the day I hit him on the head with a hoe, although the exact cause of the attack has long been forgotten.

My brother always seemed to know the one thing that would make me absolutely furious. My memory of the scenario is usually the same: our parents would go out for the evening, leaving behind a list of chores to be completed—rooms to clean, grass to mow, homework to finish. As the more compulsive son, I would assume that the tasks had to be finished immediately. My brother was much more content to take it easy. I would shout, "We have to get to work!" He would respond, "If you don't do it, it won't get done." It made my blood boil. In fact, I may remember why I hit him with the hoe!

"If you don't do it, it won't get done." I instinctively knew that he was wrong; I should not have to do it all by myself. But a deeper part of me, a part of my personality no doubt forged by high parental expectations and the conviction that these children were born for some special purpose, believed it. I grew up convinced that if I didn't do it, if I didn't get my hands around it, if I didn't make it happen, it probably would not be done.

There is an element of truth to that conviction. Most of the good things that happen in this world happen because some people, somewhere, sometime, decided that if they didn't do something, nothing would get done. The church I serve, for example, did not exist a decade ago. But a few aggressive people with a vision of the future purchased the property, began knocking on doors, and put themselves on the line to bring it into existence. They went to work and got the job done.

IF YOU DON'T DO IT...

But there is also a negative side of this conviction. Those of us who tend to be compulsive overachievers begin to believe that it all depends on us; we are the only persons who can accomplish the task.

At this point, Jacob is just like many of us. He built the first half of his life on the assumption that if he didn't do it, if he didn't make it happen, if he didn't hammer things together with his own energy and strength, it probably would not happen at all. That conviction became the driving, controlling influence in his life.

The storytellers of the Old Testament are ruthlessly honest. They never try to clean up their characters or make plaster saints out of the fathers and mothers of the faith. As I read the story of Jacob in Genesis, I even feel that this storyteller had a sense of humor. I can almost hear him saying, "Can you believe this guy?" He does not hesitate to let us know that Jacob was a cheat, a crook, a sniveling manipulator who makes J. R. Ewing look like a volunteer for the Peace Corps.

Jacob acquired his identity even before he was born:

> Rebecca became pregnant. She was going to have twins, and before they were born, they struggled against each other in her womb. She said, "Why should something like this happen to me?" So she went to ask the Lord for an answer. The Lord said to her,
> "Two nations are within you;
> You will give birth to two rival peoples.
> One will be stronger than the other;
> The older will serve the younger."
> The time came for her to give birth, and she had twin sons. The first was reddish, and his skin was like a hairy robe, so he was named Esau. The second one was born holding on tightly to the heel of Esau, so he was named Jacob.
> —25:21-26, TEV

Jacob means "heel holder" or "supplanter." Figuratively, the word paints the picture of someone who goes after the one ahead of him to try to take his place by trickery or deceit. They called him "Jacob," the deceiver, and the identity stuck.

Time passes; the boys are older now. The next time we see the twins, Esau, the outdoorsman, is coming in from hunting and is very hungry. He finds his brother cooking bean soup. Esau says, "I'm starving! Give me some of that red bean soup."

Instantly, Jacob sees his opportunity. He replies, "I will give it to you if you give me your rights as the firstborn son." He offers something to satisfy Esau's bodily hunger if Esau will give him that intangible gift of the firstborn, the blessing to be passed on in the generations of Abraham.

Esau is not the brightest bulb that was ever turned into a socket. He is portrayed as one of those persons whose attention is almost entirely on things that are physical, things that can be touched and felt. When his stomach growls, his top priority becomes satisfying it. "I am about to die from hunger. What good will my rights do me?" With the smell of bean soup in his nostrils, he gives his birthright to his brother. Jacob feeds him the soup and Esau leaves. Jacob knows how to play on his brother's weakness and thus bilks him out of his birthright. The Genesis writer then adds this postscript: "That was all Esau cared about his rights as the first-born son" (25:34, TEV).

Having swindled his twin brother, Jacob turns his attention to his father, with some direct help from his mother. Isaac is old and blind. The child of the covenant, the child rescued from sacrifice, is now gray haired, bent, blurry eyed, unable to see who is coming in the door, drooling at the mouth, yesterday's soup drying in his beard. He

IF YOU DON'T DO IT . . .

figures he is about to die. It is several more chapters until he actually gets around to dying, but Isaac thinks it is about time. "Esau," he says, "you see that I am old and may die soon. Take your bow and arrows, go out into the country, and kill an animal for me. Cook me some of that tasty food that I like, and bring it to me. After I've eaten it, I'll give you my final blessing before I die" (27:2-4, TEV). Esau heads off into the country to go hunting.

Rebecca, hiding behind the tent flap, overhears the conversation and is not above helping her favorite child. She calls Jacob and says, "Now's your chance. I'll fix some food just the way your father likes it. He can't see you anyway. You go in there and give him the dinner, he'll think you're Esau, and you'll get his blessing."

Jacob may be a crook, but he isn't a dummy. He says, "You know that Esau is a hairy man, but I have smooth skin. Perhaps my father will touch me and find out that I am deceiving him" (27:11-12, TEV). His mother tells him not to worry about that. They can use some goat skins to cover his arms and neck. When the old man touches him, he will think he is touching Esau.

They set up the trick. Jacob takes the food to his father. Isaac isn't stupid. He asks, "Which of my sons are you?" Jacob answers, "I'm your older son, Esau. I have done as you told me to. Sit up and eat. I've brought you the meat you asked me to prepare." Isaac asks, "How did you find it so quickly, son?" Jacob responds, "The Lord God helped me find it" (27:18-20).

Isaac calls to him, "Please come closer so I can touch you. Are you really Esau?" Jacob moves closer to his father. Isaac says, "Your voice sounds like Jacob, but your arms feel like Esau's arms. Are you really Esau?" Again Jacob replies, "I am." Isaac says, "Bring me the meat." And Jacob comes up close to him. Isaac smells his clothes, and so he says, "The pleasant smell of my son is like the smell of a field which the Lord has blessed" (27:27, TEV). That is quite a mouthful when you think where Esau is supposed to have been!

Isaac lays his hand on Jacob's head and says, "May God give you dew from heaven and make your fields fertile! May he give you plenty of grain and wine! May nations be your servants, and may peoples bow down before you. May you rule over your relatives, and may your mother's descendants bow down before you. May those who curse you be cursed, and may those who bless you be blessed" (27:28-29, TEV). The blessing was given and could never be taken back.

Jacob leaves the tent just as Esau enters. Esau and Isaac suddenly realize they have been duped and there is nothing that can be done. Esau cries, "This is the second time he cheated me! No wonder his name is Jacob! He took my rights as the firstborn son, and now he has taken away my blessing" (27:36). Isaac has to give Esau a secondhand blessing, and at the end of this part of the story, the writer records, "Esau hated Jacob, because his father had given Jacob the blessing. He thought, 'The time to mourn my father's death is near; then I will kill Jacob' " (27:41, TEV).

Mama comes to the rescue again. Rebecca tells Jacob to skip town. He finds himself alone in the wilderness. Night comes. He lies down to sleep and begins to dream. He dreams of a ladder, a ramp, a stairway, connecting heaven and earth, with angels going up and down the ramp. Then he hears the Lord beside him saying, "I will not leave you until all that I have promised has been fulfilled." Jacob wakes up and shouts, "The Lord is here! He's in this place, and I didn't know it. This is the house of God—the gateway to heaven" (28:15-17).

I wonder how many of us are like Jacob: absolutely convinced that we have to squeeze life together, to force, forge, and shape it by the power of our hands? We are willing to do just about anything to get the job done, to make it happen. Perhaps we, too, need to find our way to Bethel, to the place where we, with Jacob, see a ladder stretched from heaven to earth and hear the voice of the Lord beside us saying, "I am with you until I have fulfilled everything that I have promised for your life." Now and then we need to wake up with Jacob and discover that the Lord is *here*. This world, this life, these relationships, these circumstances—*this* is the house of God. *This* is where God's will is being fulfilled. *This* world is where the Lord is present, not on some far-off, ethereal plane, but right here in the stony reality of the world in which we find ourselves. This is the house of God. This is where God's purpose will be fulfilled.

As I was working on this chapter, I visited two preacher friends in Miami, which has become a front line of mission. It is a tough place to serve, a demanding place for the church to be in ministry. One of these friends served in a very rough part of the city.

His church was burglarized numerous times. Some friends came to his house for dinner and were mugged between the front door and the car. The last year he was there he received threatening phone calls. He has moved now, and I asked, "Are you glad to be out of there?" He said, "I discovered that I had two choices. Either I could go crazy, or I could learn to pray. I decided that rather than go crazy, I'd start to pray." He said that it was there he discovered the spiritual discipline to help him realize that God was present with him.

The other pastor serves a church that a generation ago was a leading church in the state, but like most downtown, inner-city churches, it has faced its share of ups and downs, changes and difficulties across the years. When he was appointed there, some persons questioned the future of that church. The bishop shared his vision. He could see that church again being the leading voice of the gospel in the major Florida city. He envisioned it filled again.

My friend headed off to Miami convinced he could do it, convinced that he could go in there, turn that thing around, and make it move again. By the end of the first year, however, he had discovered that he could not do it. He told me he discovered that if anything new and fresh was going to happen there, Christ would have to do it, and the best thing he could do would be to be available to do his part in Christ's work.

He is still working very hard, but the difference between the first year and the second year is that the first year he thought he had to do it all by himself. The second year he knew that God was doing it and was using him. He had learned the lesson Jacob learned in his dream.

Jacob awoke. He rubbed the sleep from his eyes, stretched his arms to relieve the pain in his neck, and said, "The Lord is here! The Lord is in this place, and I didn't know it." He walked into the new dawn with a new realization that God was with him and would fulfill God's purpose in his life. And we, if we are open to God's spirit, can make the same discovery. The Lord is here! The Lord is in this place. We are not alone.

A recent John Updike novel, *Roger's Version*, is the story of an ambitious young man who is convinced that he can prove the existence of God with his computer. He shares his vision with a jaded theologian who is not at all convinced of the young man's proposal.

> The young man said, "You're being satirical. But do you know why you're being satirical?"
>
> "A, I am? And B, No."
>
> "Because you're afraid. You don't *want* God to break through. People in general don't want that. They just want to grub along being human, and dirty, and sly, and amus-

IF YOU DON'T DO IT . . .

ing, and having their weekends with Michelob, and God to stay put in the churches if they ever decide to drop by, and maybe to pull them out in the end, down that tunnel of light all these [Near Death Experiences] talk about."

Would we rather "grub along being human, and dirty, and sly, and amusing," than live as if we actually expected God to break through in our real world? Would we prefer to go it alone, attempting to do it ourselves, rather than wake up to the realization that the Lord is here?

Where did you first hear of "Jacob's Ladder"? I learned it through a song, sung around the camp fires, on "Vesper Hill" or in the "Green Cathedral" at summer youth camps.

> We are climbing Jacob's ladder. . . .
> Every round goes higher, higher. . . .
> Soldiers of the cross.

It is a great old song. It was, however, two decades later that I discovered that Jacob's vision has nothing to do with our climbing up to God. It is exactly the opposite. It is the picture of the God who comes to us; the God who meets us in our wilderness, our confusion, our conflict, our doubt; the God who comes down into the real circumstances in which we find ourselves and who, by the mystery of grace, begins to work out the divine purpose in our earthly lives. Almost any place can be the place where we learn to say, "Surely the Lord is in this place, and I didn't know it!"

CHAPTER EIGHT

Wrestling in the Dark, Limping Toward the Dawn

> Looking at God, we see that we do not have him as an object of our knowledge, but that he has us as the subject of our existence. . . . We may not comprehend, but we are comprehended. We may not grasp anything in the depth of our uncertainty, but that we are grasped by something ultimate, which keeps us in its grasp and from which we may strive in vain to escape, remains absolutely certain.
>
> —Paul Tillich

READ GENESIS 29–33

Have you ever wished for a "new you"? In his letter to the Christians in Corinth, St. Paul makes this staggering affirmation: "When anyone is joined to Christ, he is a new being; the old is gone, the new has come" (2 Cor. 5:17, TEV). I suspect that if most of us were really honest with ourselves, we would be forced to admit that sometimes we wish those words were true for us.

If the psychologists, the therapists, and the people who take surveys for the magazines you pick up at the grocery store checkout counter are even close to being correct in their evaluation of the psyche of America today, most of us some of the time and some of us most of the time are searching for a new identity. We are wrestling with old things that we would like to see pass away—old attitudes, prejudices, fears, and habits keeping us from being all we would like to be. We are reaching out for something new—new goals, ambitions, dreams, a new sense of self-worth. We are like caterpillars who are fed up with our crusty, confining cocoons, struggling to break free and fly into the future with new wings. Wouldn't you like to find a new you: the "you" that God intended you to be in creation?

The story of Jacob is the story of a man who wrestled with a new identity. It is a drama of a man for whom the old began to pass away, the new began to become a reality.

As we discovered in the first half of his story, Jacob was a crook, a cheat, a manipulator, who found a way to twist every situation to his own advantage. Frederick Buechner describes him as a man who was never satisfied: "He wanted the moon, and if he'd ever managed to bilk Heaven out of that, he would have been back the next morning for the stars to go with it." Having cheated his brother of his birthright and his father of his blessing, he operates on the principle that there is no problem so big or so complicated that it cannot be solved by running away. To save his own skin, he runs off to work for his uncle, Laban.

What happens in Genesis 29–31 is an X-rated story that you probably wouldn't believe if I told it to you! It involves two wives, two concubines, eleven children, and some questionable experiments in animal husbandry. After twenty years, Jacob has ended up owning just about everything that isn't tied down on Uncle Laban's farm. Then the Lord instructs Jacob, "Go back to the land of

WRESTLING IN THE DARK, LIMPING TOWARD THE DAWN

your fathers and to your relatives. I will be with you" (31:3, TEV).

Go back? You've got to be kidding! Going back home meant that Jacob would have to deal with his past. He would have to reckon with his brother, Esau, who had threatened to kill him. He would have to face his father, Isaac, whom he had deceived. He would have to acknowledge his identity and be forced to come to grips with all that he had been.

Jacob's own voice, the memory of who he had been, the shadow of what he had done, begins to close in on him. He discovers that although he can run from Esau, he cannot run from himself. He begins the long journey back home.

For many of us, the discovery of a new identity may involve a retracing of the paths our lives have followed, a bold confrontation with the ghosts of the past, an honest look into the mirror of memory, to sort out who we have been and what we have done.

One Sunday morning after hearing Jacob's story, a young man asked if he could talk with me. He was waiting in my office when I came in from shaking hands, turning off the air conditioning, and locking the doors of the sanctuary. In a few words he described exactly what was going on in his life. Then he said, "I realized that there is a letter I need to write, a letter I've been thinking about for a long time." Before he could move any farther into his future, he had to deal with that piece of his past.

So Jacob begins his journey home. We pick up the story on the night before he is to meet Esau. He sends his entourage across the Jabbok River, but he remains behind. While he is alone in the darkness, one comes and wrestles with him until daybreak.

The Genesis storyteller is mysteriously vague about the identity of Jacob's opponent. Was it God? Was it Esau?

JOURNEYS WITH THE PEOPLE OF GENESIS

Was it Isaac? Was it Jacob himself, wrestling in a schizophrenic nightmare? Or perhaps his situation was like that of St. Paul, revealed in his moving, autobiographical statement: "I do not understand what I do; for I don't do what I would like to do, but instead I do what I hate. . . . I don't do the good I want to do; instead, I do the evil that I do not want to do. . . . What an unhappy man I am! Who will rescue me from this body that is taking me to death?" (Rom. 7:15, 19, 24, TEV). Or was it like any of us when we wrestle in the darkness of our own souls with who we have been and who we would like to become? Was it like any of us who struggle with the awesome mystery of ourselves, our relationship with God, and our relationships with others?

The experience is as old as Jacob wrestling at Peniel, as magnificent as Hamlet asking, "To be, or not to be," as contemporary as Luke Skywalker struggling with his identity as the son of Darth Vader in *Star Wars*. We find it throughout the history of literature because we find it written into the pages of our own experience. In *The Man Who Wrestled with God*, John Sanford describes this common reality when he writes, "Everyone who wrestles with his spiritual and psychological experience, and, no matter how dark or frightening it is, refuses to let it go until he discovers its meaning, is having something of the Jacob experience. Such a person can come through his dark struggle to the other side reborn, but one who retreats or runs from his encounter with spiritual reality cannot be transformed."

Whatever else this wonderfully mysterious story may mean, it speaks to one of my concerns in response to some of the slaphappy, carbonated-fizz, health-spa-for-the-soul religion that has become so popular in the eighties; the folks who promise "happiness all the time, wonderful peace of mind, since I found the Lord." I sometimes wonder if they have ever read the Old Testament.

Jacob's life was much simpler when he thought he was in control; when he was twisting, squeezing, manipulating the world to serve his own purpose; when he thought that God was up in heaven and he was down here on earth to slug it out in his own strength. But after his dream at Bethel, after he saw the ladder connecting heaven and earth, after he discovered that God was here, involved in the stony realities of his own life, everything became infinitely more complicated. The wrestling in his soul was because the God who walked beside him had begun to probe into his conscience, to disturb his personality, to break through the defenses he had so carefully built around himself. Jacob was forced to deal with questions he did not want to answer, to wrestle with things he wanted to avoid.

Several years ago a man told me that his life had become much more complicated since he became involved in our congregation. He said that before he came to the church, he could think, act, vote, spend his money, and use his talents and time just about any way he desired. But when he began to take his faith more seriously, he began to ask questions he had never asked before. Questions like: What would God have me do in this situation? How does the gospel influence the way I use my resources? What difference would the love of Christ make in this relationship? What does my faith have to do with how I respond to a particular social, economic, or political issue? He discovered that life is often infinitely more complex when we begin to live and act on the awareness that God is present with us in our daily lives.

That man discovered that the life of faith may be better, but it may not be easier; it may be healthier, but it may not be more comfortable; it may be deeper, but it may also be more demanding. But he also discovered something he could not live without. When he and his wife were preparing to move from our community, he told me that their top priority was to find a church family that would help them grow in their faith the way this one did.

More recently I received a letter from a woman who had shared with me her struggle to find God's direction for her life.

> It isn't an easy, peaceful thing to do because even though we have faith that God will provide, we have been programmed to take action, be responsible, etc. Don't we tend to view people who aren't solving their problems as lazy, avoiding the issues?
>
> For me, these past two months have been extremely torturous. Since I came to you and committed myself to finding a job that God wanted for me, I have been wrestling with myself much as Jacob did—why wasn't *I* doing more (it was God's hand restraining me); I thought I wouldn't find anything (my timing vs. God's). And now, even as these wonderful options have materialized, I am wrestling with choosing God's will. There is little peace in being led for those of us conscientious, responsible, overachievers. . . . Faith, yes; peace, no.

Both pilgrims experienced the same inner struggle described so powerfully in the images of this story from Genesis. They discovered what it means to wrestle in the darkness of their own soul, even as Jesus wrestled with his destiny in the temptation (Luke 4:1-13) and again in the garden (Luke 22:39-46).

Finding the "new you," the "you" God always intended for you to be, will involve that kind of wrestling in the darkness; but for Jacob, it also included the restoring of relationships.

WRESTLING IN THE DARK, LIMPING TOWARD THE DAWN

The entire drama revolves around the conflict, the alienation between these brothers. It builds toward the confrontation as Jacob tries to soften Esau's anger by sending messengers and gifts ahead of him. Finally the morning dawns when they are to meet for the first time in twenty years. Then comes one of the greatest surprises recorded in the Old Testament.

Jacob makes his way toward Esau expecting the worst, bowing to the ground in humility as he approaches his brother. "But Esau ran to meet him, threw his arms around him, and kissed him. They were both crying" (33:4, TEV). Reconciled with his brother, Jacob says, "To see your face is for me like seeing the face of God, now that you have been so friendly to me" (33:10, TEV).

For Jacob, seeing the face of God involved looking his brother in the eye. He learned a lesson that we, in our overly individualized society, too easily forget: we cannot be right with God and be wrong with our brothers and sisters. Reconciliation with God is woven into our relationships with people around us.

I'm not sure how we manage to miss this truth. Jesus made it perfectly clear. He said that if we bring a gift to the altar and remember that our brother or sister has something against us, we should first go and be made right with the brother or sister. Then we are ready to lay our gift on the altar.

In the prayer Jesus taught us to pray, we say, "Forgive us our trespasses as we forgive those who trespass against us." The necessity of reconciliation comes across even stronger when Jesus adds, "If you forgive others the wrongs they have done, your Father in heaven will also forgive you; but if you do not forgive others, then the wrongs you have done will not be forgiven by your Father" (Matt. 6:14-15, NEB).

St. John picked up on this theme when he wrote, "If

someone says he loves God, but hates his brother, he is a liar. For he cannot love God, whom he has not seen, if he does not love his brother, whom he has seen. The command that Christ has given us is this: whoever loves God must love his brother also" (1 John 4:20-21, TEV). If you want to find the new you, you will probably be involved in restoring relationships with others.

A friend recently introduced me to a novel entitled *The Shooting Party* by Isabel Colgate. It is set in England at the end of the nineteenth century and tells the story of a fascinating collection of people who are invited to a country estate for a week of hunting, dining, and relaxing in the elegant style of the aristocracy. As you would expect, a man and a woman, both of whom are married, are attracted to each other. As you would expect, the man begins to move the relationship toward intimacy. You would expect the next step to be passionate lovemaking. But that is where the surprise comes in the story. The woman says, "No." When was the last time you heard anyone say no on television or in the movies? She explains her denial by saying, "But we have to live in the real world, a world with other people in it, not a dream world, with only us."

Jacob learned that he had to live in a real world, a world with Esau and Isaac in it, a world in which he could not find himself outside his relationships with others.

In their study of individualism and commitment in American life, *Habits of the Heart*, Robert Bellah and his team came to this conclusion about our contemporary desire to "find ourselves":

> We believe that much of the thinking about the self of educated Americans . . . is based on inadequate social science, impoverished philosophy, and vacuous theology. There are truths we do not see when we adopt the lan-

guage of radical individualism. We find ourselves not independently of other people and institutions but through them. We never get to the bottom of our selves on our own. We discover who we are face to face and side by side with others in work, love, and learning. . . . We are not simply ends in ourselves, either as individuals or as a society. We are parts of a larger whole that we can neither forget nor imagine in our own image without paying a high price. If we are not to have a self that hangs in the void, slowly twisting in the wind, these are issues we cannot ignore.

They are calling us to relearn the lesson Jacob learned at Peniel.

It would be tempting to leave the story there, with Jacob and Esau riding off into the sunset to live happily ever after, except for one thing: Jacob's limp, the consequence of the long night of wrestling. The storyteller says that they wrestled all night long, and in the morning, when the opponent could see that he was not winning, he hit Jacob in the hip so that it was thrown out of joint, which was just the kind of dirty trick that old Jacob would have tried! The story of the wrestling match concludes with these words: "The sun rose as Jacob was leaving Peniel, and he was limping because of his hip" (32:31, TEV).

Jacob received his new identity: "Your name will no longer be Jacob. . . . your name will be Israel" (32:28, TEV). His inner nature was changed. His personal identity reformed, he was given a new future, but he moved off toward the dawn limping all the way. It was the indelible sign of the struggle he had endured.

As I held the picture of the limping Jacob in my mind, I recalled one of my favorite stories of the risen Christ. The setting is the upper room. The disciples are all gathered together. The risen Christ appears. When Thomas asks for some evidence that Jesus is really alive, what sign does

Jesus give? He shows him the print of the nails in his hands; he lets him feel the scar of the sword in his side.

In sign language for the deaf, the sign for *Jesus* is to point with the third finger of one hand to the palm of the other and vice versa. The risen Christ is identified by the nail scars in his hands.

There is a profound mystery here. Even the risen Christ does not come to new life without the scars, the wounds, the marks of his struggle in the darkness. Instead of being wiped away by some sort of divine plastic surgery, those scars become the evidence of his risen life. The wounds left by his suffering, defeat, and death on the cross become the identifying marks of God's goodness and love.

Charles Colson was the "hatchet man" in the Nixon White House, a man at the vortex of power and authority, but he was convicted and sent to prison for his involvement in the Watergate scandal. Along the way he became a Christian. The validity of his conversion has been proven by his leadership in prison ministry.

Colson has said that the thing that amazes him the most about how God has used his life is the realization that God did not choose to use his strengths—his law degree, his political influence, his clout in Washington. God has chosen to use his weakness. God has taken the greatest defeat in Charles Colson's life and used it in a redemptive way. He has taken the scar of Colson's identity as a convicted felon and has used it for the sake of others. Charles Colson received a new identity, but he received it with a limp, the identifying mark of the God who takes our weakness and transforms it into strength, who takes our failure and turns it into victory.

Would you like to find the "new you"—the "you" that God intends for you to become? Would you like to see something old pass away so that something new can come? Many of us will discover that new identity by

WRESTLING IN THE DARK, LIMPING TOWARD THE DAWN

wrestling in the dark, by finding ourselves in restored relationships, and by limping into the dawn. Then we will hear the Spirit say, "Your name is Israel because you have wrestled with God and with man and have prevailed."

CHAPTER NINE

The Best Thing About Growing Old

> I know that Jesus walks with us along our pilgrim journey, but doesn't have us in harness or on a leash, for God tenders maximum support but minimum protection.
>
> —William Sloane Coffin

READ GENESIS 35:1-15

I'm sure you've heard some of the one-liners about getting older.

You know you're getting old when everything hurts and what doesn't hurt doesn't work.

You know you're getting old when your back goes out more than you do.

You know you're getting old when your knees buckle and your belt won't.

You know you're getting old when you feel like the

morning after the night before and you haven't been anywhere.

You know you're getting old when you sink your teeth into a good steak and leave them there.

To listen to some people talk, you would get the impression that the only good thing about old age is that it beats the alternative.

Chapter 35 of Genesis, however, records Jacob's journey back to the land of his beginnings and points to something that can make getting older one of the best things in life. Like a retired baseball player who can't stay away from the park, he makes his way back to Bethel, back to the place where he had his vision of the ladder connecting heaven and earth, the place where he discovered that he wasn't down here on his own to slug it out under his own power, the place he discovered that God was here beside him, involved in the realities of his life.

Listen to how he describes the purpose of the journey: "We are going to . . . Bethel, where I will build an altar to the God who helped me in the time of my trouble and who has been with me everywhere I have gone" (35:3, TEV).

One of the best things about growing older is the opportunity to look back along all the winding paths our lives have followed, to thumb through the pictures we have pasted into the scrapbook of memory, and to say with Jacob, "Look at this! Look at the way the Lord has helped us in our trouble! God has been with us all the way!"

When you think about it, this affirmation was quite a strong one for Jacob. His life's journey had been no idyllic tale told with gentle strings playing soft music in the background. It was the rough-and-tumble story of a man who wrestled with himself, with God, and with others. It was the story of a man who struggled with difficult choices, sometimes not at all sure he was doing the correct thing, sometimes fully aware that he was not. His life was complicated by tangled relationships with his brother, his father, and his uncle, to say nothing of his two wives, two concubines, and eleven children. Even the sordid story of the rape of his daughter is included in Genesis. When he returned to Bethel, he did not look back on a smooth, easygoing life.

And yet, he builds an altar and celebrates, offering wine and olive oil to the God who helped him in trouble and was with him all the way. For Jacob and for many of us, it is only when we look back across the road we have traveled that we can see clearly how the Lord has been with us.

I hear some people say that they know with absolute clarity exactly what God wants them to do. I rejoice with them in that confidence, but I must admit that most of the time I find myself attempting to make the best decisions I know how to make, praying that God is leading in that choice, but not at all sure that it was correct until one day I look back and say, "Lo and behold, the Lord was with me all the way!"

It is helpful to observe what Jacob did *not* say. He did not say, "The God who gave me everything I ever wanted." He did not say, "The God who saved me from every danger, protected me from every injury, rescued me from every problem, kept me from every disease." He did not say, "The God who made my life smooth and easy." He offered his sacrifice to "the God who helped me in the time of my trouble and who has been with me everywhere I have gone." That was enough for Jacob; perhaps it should be enough for us, too.

On the first Sunday morning when I was in Nairobi, Kenya, still groggy from the effects of jet lag, I rolled out of bed and found my way to All Saints' Cathedral for morning worship. By the time I found my way through the city on foot, the nave was already full. The only seat I could find was directly behind one of the massive stone pillars supporting the roof of the typically British structure. Unable to see the altar, I listened not only to the preacher, not only to the singing of traditional Anglican chants and gospel songs to an African beat, but also to myself, feeling strangely alone as one of a small handful of white persons in the congregation and yet strangely at home, as if I belonged there, too.

The offertory hymn was from the pen of Joseph Addison, who scanned the horizon of his own life and wrote,

> When all thy mercies, O my God,
> My rising soul surveys,
> Transported with the view, I'm lost
> In wonder, love, and praise.
> Unnumbered comforts to my soul
> Thy tender care bestowed,
> Before my infant heart could know
> From whom those comforts flowed.
> When in the slippery paths of youth
> With heedless steps I ran,
> Thine arm, unseen, conveyed me safe,
> And led me up to man.
> Through every period of my life
> Thy goodness I'll pursue;
> And after death, in distant worlds,
> The glorious theme renew.

As I sang that hymn, my mind raced back across the ocean and across the years in a rapid review of my life—opportunities, relationships, choices that had been used by God to bring me to that moment. The young Kenyan family beside me probably wondered why I stopped singing to catch the lump in my throat. As I placed my offering in the velvet pouchlike basket, I rejoiced with the poet and said to myself, "That's my song, too!"

I am confident that the emotion I felt during the offering in Nairobi is the same emotion Jacob felt as he prepared his offering at Bethel: the awesome awareness of the undeserved goodness and mercy of the God who had been with him all the way.

If you turn Jacob's affirmation inside out and look at it from a different perspective, you discover that the God Jacob honored at Bethel was the God who, from Jacob's mother's womb, saw the identity Jacob should have and kept that identity in mind through the long procession of questions, doubts, blunders, and circumstances of his life. The result was that when he came back to Bethel, he had, in fact, "come home" to the identity God had always intended for him.

John W. Donohue, writing in "America," celebrated the life, faith, and conversion of British actor Sir Alec Guinness. He said that in Guinness's life we can see "how a multi-layered twentieth-century life integrated work, art, friendships, family relationships and religious faith." Not a small accomplishment when you think of it! He reports that in the mid-1950s Guinness, his wife, and their son, somewhat independently of one another, found themselves drawn into the Catholic church. Guinness said, "Like countless converts before and after me, I felt I had come home. . . . There had been no emotional upheaval, no great insight, certainly no proper grasp of theological issues; just a sense of history and the fittingness of things."

Donohue compared this to Scottish novelist George MacDonald, who described the "new name" that expresses God's own idea of the person to whom that name is given, "that being whom [God] had in His thought when He began to make the child, and whom He kept in His thought through the long process that went to realize the idea."

The story of Jacob points us toward faith in the God who had something in mind for Jacob from the time he struggled in Rebecca's womb and who kept that identity in view through the long and difficult process by which Jacob became the person God intended him to be, until he "came home" to Bethel when he poured his wine and olive oil over the altar to the God who helped him in his time of trouble and had been with him everywhere he had gone.

I wish I could promise that you will always know ahead of time what God intends for you. I wish I could promise that if you choose to live by faith, you will always be led down a clear path toward God's will for your life with no questions, doubts, mistakes, fears, conflicts, or pain. I cannot promise that. But I can promise that if you take up your journey and follow it as honestly and as faithfully as you can by the light that you are given, someday, somewhere, you will be able to sing with Jacob, "The Lord has helped me in my trouble! The Lord has been with me all the way."

CHAPTER TEN

Don't Forget Joseph

He who, from zone to zone,
Guides through the boundless sky thy certain flight,
In the long way that I must tread alone,
Will lead my steps aright.

—William Cullen Bryant

READ GENESIS 37

I am blessed by being included in a circle of seven friends I affectionately call my cronies. We meet twice a year for three days of laughter, sharing, study, prayer, and fun. Last December we were offered the use of an oceanfront condominium. As we listened to the waves roll in on the shore and felt the brisk winter wind blow in from the Atlantic, doors were opened into deep places of our souls where we entered with trust and affirmation.

I shared a long-standing anxiety about the possibility of being asked to move from my present position in my church. What would happen if I were gone? Would the congregation continue to grow? Would the people to whom I have given so much of myself hang in there with a new pastor? Would the potential we have seen so clearly be fulfilled? After wrestling with those anxieties for some time, one of my soul brothers, who earned a Ph.D. in Old Testament studies, leaned back, scratched his head, and said, "Now, Jim, sometimes you have to trust the providence of God. Don't forget about Joseph."

Who could forget Joseph? The story comprising the final quarter of the Book of Genesis—more space than is given to any other single character—is one of the best short stories ever written. It contains all the human emotions of jealousy, fear, injustice, sexual desire, hope, and faith in a powerful drama that can hold its own with Shakespeare in its suspense and power.

It carries a different theme or perspective from what we have seen so far. Whereas the stories of Abraham, Isaac, and Jacob move with a passionate sense of God's direct interaction, each human character forced to make difficult choices in response to the call of God, Joseph's story shows God's hiddenness in the affairs of people and nations. God does not speak directly to Joseph, calling him to go to the Promised Land or take his son to Mount Moriah. God does not wrestle with Joseph in the wilderness until a new identity is born. Rather, the Joseph story points to the silent working of God in the circumstances of history. It is the story of the "God of the long haul" who ultimately accomplishes the divine purpose, though it may come as a surprise to those who are involved in it.

There is no direct appeal to faith, no outright demand for obedience, no clear call to action. Rather, this tale of fortune and misfortune emerges as an expression of faith in the God who is present within the twisting paths of human history, where freedom of choice often changes the terrain, to move the world toward the fulfillment of

Hyksos ruled Egypt
Semites 1500-1600 BC

DON'T FORGET JOSEPH

God's good purpose first revealed in creation, then renewed in the covenant.

Although considerable debate surrounds the origin of this story, some scholars place it during the rule of Solomon in the tenth century B.C. as an attempt to explain the ways of God in the history of the people of Israel. The facts were clear: the people of Israel had found their way to the Promised Land. The next thing we know, they are slaves in Egypt. That is, in fact, where we leave them at the close of Genesis. Where was God in all of this? Could they trust God's purpose to be fulfilled? How is God at work in the choices of others that directly affect the lives and history of the people of the covenant?

As you experience Joseph's story, watch for two basic themes to emerge. First is the hiddenness of God. Although never directly seen, seldom heard, and often denied, God is silently present, weaving the events of Joseph's life into a purposeful whole. James Russell Lowell, in "Once to Every Man and Nation," described that truth so well:

> Though the cause of evil prosper,
> Yet 'tis truth alone is strong;
> Though her portion be the scaffold,
> And upon the throne be wrong:
> Yet that scaffold sways the future,
> And, behind the dim unknown,
> Standeth God within the shadow
> Keeping watch above his own.

The second theme is that God's purpose will triumph in spite of the contradictory actions of others, and sometimes in spite of the actions of Joseph himself. To live by faith means that we continue to believe God's way will be

Hound of the Heavens

JOURNEYS WITH THE PEOPLE OF GENESIS

victorious, even when the circumstances of history seem to contradict it.

D. T. Niles, the leader of the YMCA in India and a spiritual giant of this century, recounted in his book, *The Power at Work Among Us*, "During the darkest days of the German occupation of Norway, Bishop Berggrav said, 'God is preparing a victory in the night.' " Wrote Niles, "He knew nothing about the preparations going on in England for the invasion of Normandy, but he knew his God."

I discovered the same faith tucked away as a postscript to a sermon by a preacher who was never known beyond the Illinois congregations he served and the tiny Florida community in which he retired. His name was Albert Belyea. I found him in Crescent City, Florida, in retirement. He immediately became my pastor, counselor, and friend. When he died, his wife gave me most of his books and a box full of his sermons.

Every now and then I pull a couple of the sermons out of the pile and read them. Typed single-space on yellowing pages, they are the living words of a pastor who loved his people and preached to their needs. This is particularly true of the sermons from the days of World War II. Many of them deal with faith, with titles like "Daring to Trust God" and "Faith to Believe." In a sermon preached just after Franklin Roosevelt died and Harry Truman became president, he concluded with this affirmation: "Folks disbelieve today, but God is not defeated. Let men make their promises and break them with impunity . . . but God is the same yesterday, today and forever, and in the end his way will win. . . . That is great good news we need to proclaim to a confused, frightened, suffering world. God is still with us. In the end his will will triumph."

The typed manuscript ended there, but handwritten

beneath it, as if personally addressed to me, I found these words: "Eventually the world will be redeemed. You and I will not see it, nevertheless, it will come to pass." To live by faith is to place our confidence in the ultimate triumph of the sometimes hidden God and to live as if we expect God's will to be fulfilled.

One of my best college memories is our campus production of Rodgers and Hammerstein's masterpiece, *The Sound of Music*. The performance I remember most vividly was an afternoon matinee for the children of the local elementary school. Busing three hundred children to the campus was a major logistical accomplishment in and of itself! By the time they were seated in the auditorium, we were forty-five minutes late getting the curtain up. In their spontaneity and imagination, the children were immediately drawn into the production. They laughed, clapped, and responded openly to everything that happened on stage. The problem was that their responses slowed down the production even more. By the end of the first act, it became obvious that the chances of getting the Von Trapp family to the mountain before the buses arrived at the doors to carry the children away were very, very thin. Throughout the second act, my assistant director and I were backstage, ruthlessly cutting, chopping, and putting the script back together to get the main story in and still come out on time.

On stage were some very confused actors and actresses. They were never sure what tune the orchestra would play next. When they least expected it, someone who wasn't scheduled to appear for at least another five pages of the script would come marching in and give the opening line for a whole new scene. On stage, there were moments of total confusion, but backstage, we were taking all those changes and interruptions and putting them together in a way that would come out at the right place at the right time. It worked. We did manage to "climb every mountain" before the bus drivers started blowing their horns!

Don't forget Joseph. On stage, he will become tangled in all sorts of twists in the plot, affected by other people's choices that shift the direction of the story. There are times when it looks as if Joseph's dream is headed right down the tubes. But backstage, hidden from view, the spirit of God is quietly, consistently, continuously taking all those twists, turns, and changes and working them together so that when we reach the end of the life of Joseph, the drama of God's covenant people is exactly where God wants it to be.

Don't forget Joseph. But more important, don't forget the hidden God who is working out a good purpose in his life.

CHAPTER ELEVEN

Here Comes the Dreamer!

> In the task of that redemption the most effective agents will be men who have substituted some new illusions for the abandoned ones. . . . Justice cannot be approximated if the hope of its perfect realization does not generate a sublime madness in the soul.
>
> —Reinhold Niebuhr

READ GENESIS 37–38

You could say a lot of things about Joseph. You could say that he was young, seventeen, to be exact. You could say that he was spoiled; the famous "coat of many colors" (actually, a "coat with long sleeves") was the ultimate sign of his position as the favored child. You could say that he was a tattletale who carried stories about his brothers back to Jacob. It would be an understatement to say that he had poor sibling relationships; the truth is that his brothers wanted to kill him. All these statements are true, but they are all secondary elements in the story. The most important fact that ultimately set Joseph apart from his brothers was that he had a dream (37:5).

My experience convinces me that one of the things continuing to set some people apart from the masses is that they have a dream. People who make a difference, people who survive hardship and difficulty with their personal integrity intact, people who find inner strength to face demanding times, people who are able to maintain their faith when all the circumstances around them run counter to their ideals, are people who have been possessed by a dream.

It was a cold, clear February night, cold enough to send most of the tourists in the nation's capital shivering to their hotel rooms. Only a few people were on the street as we parked our car and made our way up the long stairs ascending the front of the Lincoln Memorial. Step by step we could see more of the massive figure seated between the pillars. We walked into the Memorial and looked up into those eyes, carved in marble, that almost seem alive. A young black father and mother with a preschool-aged son stood beside me. I watched as the father lifted the boy to his shoulders so he could see more clearly. The mother pointed to the big man in the chair, telling the child who Lincoln was.

I turned to one side and read the words of the Gettysburg Address. On the other, I read the magnificent words of the Second Inaugural Address. In solitary silence, I turned and walked slowly back out onto the steps.

Stretching out before me was the Reflecting Pool, a frozen mirror creating a snow-covered bridge to the Washington Monument pointing its pure white finger into the moonless winter sky. My mind wandered back to what was, for American society, one of the most crucial events to occur in my lifetime.

HERE COMES THE DREAMER!

It was August 28, 1963. An estimated crowd of two hundred fifty thousand people who had come from all across the nation was gathered on both sides of that pool, a solid mass of humanity from one monument to the other. In the blistering afternoon sun, Martin Luther King, Jr., stood on those same steps. In my memory I could hear him proclaiming in the forceful rhythm of his speech: "In spite of the difficulties and frustrations of the moment I still have a dream."

With the voices of the congregation responding, "Tell it, Doctor!" and "Alright!" he described his dream.

> It is a dream deeply rooted in the American dream.
> I have a dream that one day this nation will rise up and live out the true meaning of its creed: "We hold these truths to be self-evident; that all men are created equal."
> I have a dream that one day on the red hills of Georgia the sons of former slaves and the sons of former slaveowners will be able to sit down together at the table of brotherhood. . . .
> I have a dream that my four little children will one day live in a nation where they will not be judged by the color of their skin but by the content of their character.

As the cold winter wind whipped across my back, I imagined the sweating crowd, swaying to the rhythm of the preacher, crying out to him, "Dream some more!"

> I have a dream that one day every valley shall be exalted, every hill and mountain shall be made low, the rough places will be made plains, and the crooked places will be made straight, and the glory of the Lord shall be revealed. . . .
> This is our hope. This is the faith. . . . With this faith we will be able to transform the jangling discords of our nation into a beautiful symphony of brotherhood. With this faith

we will be able to work together, to pray together, to struggle together, to go to jail together, to stand up for freedom together, knowing that we will be free one day.

By now the masses in my imagination had joined hands and become one body in the inspiration of the hour. As their shouts and applause began to rise, Dr. King concluded, "We . . . will be able to join hands and sing in the words of that old Negro spiritual, Free at last! Free at last! Thank God Almighty, we are free at last!"

People of faith are like that: they are prisoners of a dream, people who have been grasped by a vision of what this world can be. Never satisfied with what is, but always dreaming about what could be, they give themselves to make that dream come true.

Shakespeare said, "We are such stuff as dreams are made on," but I wonder if it isn't the other way around. Dreams are also the stuff that we are made on. Our lives are given shape, form, and substance when we find a goal worthy of our effort, a cause noble enough to deserve our commitment.

Felix and Annabelle Chappellet had it all. She was the daughter of the founder of a chain of grocery stores, and he had been a leader in the oil industry. Los Angeles society was shocked when they were found dead in the garage on their estate in a double suicide. The gardener discovered their bodies on the back seat of a Cadillac sedan after he noticed that the garage door had been sealed with rags and newspapers. The overheated car engine had stalled but not before producing enough noxious fumes to kill the seventy-three-year-old couple.

The suicides were obviously well planned. Investigators found detailed instructions on the disposal of possessions that were not included in their wills. The note ended with a tragic sentence revealing that they had no more dreams.

William Sloane Coffin calls us to recognize that "if we do not look for something above us, we soon sink to something below us, for it is hard to believe in the dreams and powers that we hardly suspect ourselves to possess." Dreams are the stuff we are made of, and without a dream, our lives begin to lose their meaning.

I entered adolescence in a time when America was strong on dreams. John Kennedy, the youngest president in our history, had just moved into the White House, which news reporters called "Camelot." He said, "The torch has been passed to a new generation." We believed that we were destined to go into "The New Frontier." We would be the generation to go to the moon, which eventually we did. We believed we would also be the generation that would bring world peace, end racial prejudice, and wipe out poverty and ignorance—we didn't.

Nearly three decades later, many of my peers are asking the question asked in the movie *The Big Chill*: Was it all just fashion? The visions have not become realities; the dreams have yet to be fulfilled. Many of the hopes of the "new generation" were shot to smithereens in Dallas, Memphis, and Viet Nam. My daughters have entered adolescence in a much more pragmatic, cynical world; a world in which the visions are smaller, the dreams are close at hand, the ideals more easily compromised.

Not long ago I watched a public television broadcast of the twenty-fifth anniversary concert by Peter, Paul and Mary, the musical group that put the dreams of the early sixties into music all of us could sing: "This Land Is Your Land," "Puff, the Magic Dragon," "Where Have All the Flowers Gone?" and "If I Had a Hammer." As I heard their voices blending in simple folk harmony again, there was a tug deep within my soul, and I knew that those adolescent dreams, tempered by experience and tested by time, are still the hopes and dreams nourishing my personality and inspiring my ministry.

They concluded the concert with the song that made them famous and that they have sung in every concert for twenty-five years, "Blowin' in the Wind." My first memory of that song goes back to the early 1960s and a conference-wide youth rally in Pittsburgh, Pennsylvania. I was in junior high school. A college-age folk-singing group (there were so many of them back then!) used that song as the theme for the day. Coming from a very conservative background in which religious questions always had crisp, clear, absolute answers, I remember thinking that it was a rather inconclusive song. It asked all those disturbing questions:

> . . . how many deaths will it take till he knows that too many people have died?
> . . . .
> . . . how many years can some people exist before they're allowed to be free?
> . . . how many times can a man turn his head pretending he just doesn't see?

Good questions. And to each one came the musical reply:

> The answer, my friend, is blowin' in the wind.
> The answer is blowin' in the wind.

When Mary Travers introduced the song in the televised concert, she looked at the audience and said, "You were and you are, and you will always be that answer that blows in the wind."

Evidently the people in the audience felt what she intended. As the cameras scanned the crowd, they caught images of balding, middle-aged men and graying women, several of them holding their small children on their knees. Years had passed for them as they had for me. The dreams had not been fulfilled; the answers still seemed elusive; but it was obvious that these folks still shared the vision of peace, justice, freedom, and harmony for our world. They swung their heads in agreement as they sang along; many wiped tears from their eyes; and when, on the last refrain, the trio built to a crescendo in double rhythm, the people rose to their feet, not only applauding the singers, but once again affirming the song—reaffirming with a deeper maturity the same commitments that had filled them with idealism so many years ago when they were the age of Joseph, the young man who had a dream. If you keep your ears open, you will hear the voices of dreamers all around you.

I heard a woman say that although her life has been filled with confusion and turbulent change brought on by a very difficult divorce, the thing that keeps her going is her conscious search for the way God can use her life constructively in this world.

I heard it from the lips of a ninety-three-year-old retired admiral who is one of the liveliest persons I know. When I asked what keeps him so young, he said, "Every night before I go to bed I ask myself this question: What have you done today that was some constructive good for the world? I get up every morning determined to accomplish some worthwhile goal during that day."

I heard it on the lips of a man who described his dream as a teenager to be a professional musician. In spite of the fact that everyone around him thought he was crazy, he went to work on that dream, accomplished his goal, and is finding joy and fulfillment in his work.

I heard it from a parent who said, "I have just one dream for my children: I want them to grow up to be Christian people who find God's will for their lives. Beyond that, whatever they want to do or become is fine with me."

The Genesis storyteller records that Joseph had a dream. But if you've read the whole story, you know that it was not really Joseph's dream, not something he "dreamed up" on his own. It was God's dream. It was the beginning of God's silent, hidden influence in the life of a spoiled, slightly arrogant, moderately overbearing adolescent boy. The dream would face tremendous resistance and create significant conflict. Joseph would be honed, tested, and refined. But one day, a long time off in a distant land, God would see that dream come true.

CHAPTER TWELVE

The Power to See It Through

Faith is not simply a patience which passively suffers until the storm is past. Rather, it is a spirit which bears things—with resignation, yes, but above all, with blazing serene hope.

—Corazon Aquino

READ GENESIS 39–41

There is no doubt about it: it's a long, long way from Broadway to Grand Lake, Colorado, and it's a long way from Radio City Music Hall to the Pine Cone Theater. The "theater" is actually a yellow-and-white-striped party tent erected for the summer at the end of Main Street, with rusted folding chairs on wooden risers, facing a small stage where a poorly tuned piano accompanies summer productions of familiar musicals and well-worn comedies. It's not much, but it's the only show in town!

We went to the theater on our second night in Grand Lake, dressed in blue jeans and sweaters in anticipation of the Rocky Mountain chill, to see *Man of La Mancha*, the story of "dreamer extraordinary," Don Quixote. Halfway through the first act, the wind began to blow, the rain began to fall, the sides of the tent began to flap in the wind, and the most ferocious storm of the summer blew in across the lake. Seated in the back row, we could barely hear the actors, our attention distracted by the rain and by the stage lights rocking back and forth, suspended between the upright tent posts. We would have considered leaving, but at least we were dry inside . . . at least, we thought, until the whole thing would collapse!

To our amazement and their credit, the actors maintained their characters, remembered their lines, and sang their songs through the storm. The male lead competed with the deluge as he sang "The Impossible Dream." All of which could be a living parable of just how difficult it can be to keep a dream alive in the storm: to maintain your personal integrity, to hold your convictions, to live by faith when life is difficult and everything seems to have turned against you.

Will Steger described this kind of endurance in his journal of the 1986 Steger International Polar Expedition to the North Pole by dogsled, a feat that had not been attempted since 1909. They traveled over four hundred miles across the polar icecap for fifty-six exhausting days. Steger told of their emotions during a particularly trying part of the journey:

> Our moods swung wildly with each change in conditions. For hours we'd fight our way through a hellish chaos of huge rubble, suddenly breaking free onto a plain that seemed endless. Despair would flash to exhilaration. "Finally the worst is behind us," we'd gasp. An hour or two later we'd strike another maze. . . . Another slump. Another heavy dose of doubt about our prospects. . . . We found ourselves expending as much precious energy fighting doubt as we did fighting pressure ridges. But now . . .

THE POWER TO SEE IT THROUGH

we've learned to stop groping for some elusive highway of smooth travel to the Pole and settle in for the long, hard grind northward.

All of us, I think, sooner or later, in small things or large, wrestle our way through the "hellish chaos" that seems to surround us until we break out onto a large plain, breathe a deep sigh of relief, and say, "Finally, the worst is behind us!"—only to discover another maze a few miles down the road, mountains of icy rubble blocking our movement toward our goal. All of us face the storms of life; therefore, all of us need to discover, as Joseph discovered in Egypt, the power to see it through, the faith to hold on when everything is working against our dreams, the courage to maintain our convictions, the strength to keep going toward what seems to be an elusive goal.

Joseph was the favorite son, born with a silver spoon in his mouth, a long-sleeved coat on his back, and great dreams in his soul. But his brothers threatened to kill him, threw him into a pit, and sold him into slavery in Egypt: a slump, a pit, a heavy dose of despair.

In Egypt things began to look up. Instead of being sold to the Greater Nile Construction Company to die building the pyramids, Joseph was purchased by a man named Potiphar, the chief of the king's guards. The Genesis storyteller records, "The Lord was with Joseph and made him successful. He lived in the house of his Egyptian master, who saw that the Lord was with Joseph and had made him successful in everything he did. . . . So he put him in charge of his house and everything he owned" (39:2-4, TEV).

Not bad for someone who started out as a slave! Things were looking up. Then he confronted Potiphar's wife, who is the biblical version of TV's Joan Collins, the real villain of the drama. "Joseph was well-built and good-looking, and after a while his master's wife began to desire Joseph and asked him to go to bed with her. He refused and said to her, 'Look, my master does not have to concern himself with anything in the house, because I am here. He has put me in charge of everything he has. . . . How then could I do such an immoral thing and sin against God?' " (39:6-9, TEV). That didn't stop Potiphar's wife, but through it all, Joseph maintained his convictions: "Although she asked Joseph day after day, he would not go to bed with her" (39:10, TEV).

Because she could not break his moral character, she turned against him, stole his coat, accused him of trying to molest her, and had him thrown into prison. Another slump; a storm; despair.

Eventually, however, things began to improve: "But the Lord was with Joseph and blessed him, so that the jailer was pleased with him. He put Joseph in charge of all the other prisoners and made him responsible for everything that was done in the prison. . . . The Lord was with Joseph and made him succeed in everything he did" (39:21-23, TEV).

In time, the king of Egypt needed to have a dream interpreted. A former prisoner remembered that Joseph had that gift. They brought Joseph out of the prison, and he interpreted the king's dream. The king of Egypt said, "We will never find a better man than Joseph, a man who has God's spirit in him." And he told Joseph, "I will put you in charge of my country, and all my people will obey your orders. Your authority will be second only to mine" (41:38, 40, TEV).

There is much more to the story, but the brief outline is enough to cause us to ask, Where did he find the power to see it through?

I respect Joseph as a young man who would not compromise his integrity for physical pleasure. He refused to trade in his long-term goals for short-term success. Call it conscience; call it character; call it integrity; label it whatever you wish, but Joseph is a model for men and women who choose to live on the basis of what they know to be God's best for their lives and will not yield to the temptation of compromise.

I remember the day I read the story of Joseph's situation with Potiphar's wife in a worship service. There were gasps of surprise and muffled giggles in the congregation. Several individuals told me they could hardly believe the story was in the Bible. It sounded like a script for the afternoon soap operas.

Remember that Joseph was between seventeen and twenty years old, a young adult at the peak of his emerging sexual desire. The writer also describes him as "well-built and good-looking." No wonder Potiphar's wife noticed him, desired him, and attempted to seduce him. Day after day she tried to wear him down. Over and over he resisted: "How can I do such a thing?"

Joseph consistently refused to compromise his convictions or to betray the trust of his master, in spite of her seduction from without and, no doubt, his own sexual desire from within. The psychological power of Joseph's temptation is even stronger when you remember that he was entirely alone, isolated from the community and family that undergirded his values, cut off from the faith of his forebears, no doubt depressed and low in spirit.

In *The Screwtape Letters*, C. S. Lewis created a collection of letters from Screwtape in hell to his nephew, Wormwood, a junior tempter on earth. In one letter, Screwtape describes the advantage of catching his subject when he is in an emotional "trough."

DEAR WORMWOOD:
   Has no one ever told you about the law of undulation?

> Humans are amphibians—half spirit and half animal. . . . While their spirit can be directed to an eternal object, their bodies, passions, and imaginations are in continual change. . . . Their nearest approach to constancy therefore, is undulation . . . a series of troughs and peaks. If you had watched your patient carefully you would have seen this undulation in every department of his life—his interest in his work, his affection for his friends, his physical appetites, all go up and down. . . . Next week I will give you some hints on how to exploit the troughs.

In his next letter, Screwtape explains. "I have always found that the Trough periods of the human undulation provide excellent opportunity for all sensual temptations. . . . The attack has a much better chance of success when the man's whole inner world is drab and cold and empty."

Potiphar's wife exploited the trough in Joseph's life. I can hear voices in our day saying, "Why not, Joseph? Go ahead, for goodness sake. Things are tough. You're lonely. So is she. Who would ever blame you? You're a healthy young man. It's natural. Go ahead."

But resisting the force of temptation both without and within, this young man consistently, gently, forcefully, denied his own desires and asked, "How could I do such a thing? How could I do this and sin against my God, my master, and myself?" He would not trade in his character for sexual satisfaction; he would not sell his integrity for comfort; he would not compromise his long-term dreams for short-term pleasures.

For Joseph, and for many people, the temptation was sexual. But for you, it may come in some other area in your life. It could be in your work or career. It may have to do with your finances, some intriguing deal that has shady corners around it. Whatever it is, Joseph stands as the model for men and women who choose to live by their highest convictions and refuse to sacrifice their integrity for the sake of short-term pleasures or short-term goals. The power to see it through is born out of that kind of integrity.

But what do you do during the long, hard grind? What do you do with your hands, your mind, your body, your talent, and your skill while you're down there in Egypt waiting for something to happen to open the way to your dream? What do you do when you keep doing the right thing, but everything keeps turning out wrong? Joseph discovered that you do the best you know how to do with the opportunity that is before you and trust the rest to God.

Over and over again the Genesis writer records, "The Lord was with him and he succeeded in all that he did," which is a strong statement when you realize that his first success was as a slave in Potiphar's house. Then it was success as a prison convict; always an alien in a foreign country.

I don't know about you, but I think if I had been Joseph, I would have given up a long time ago. As I was being carried off to Egypt, I would have become very bitter toward those brothers and shouted, "I never did anything to deserve this!" And I would have been correct. As a slave in Potiphar's house, I would have groaned, "This isn't fair!" And it wasn't. I think during those years in prison I would have been tempted to self-pity, crying, "I might as well just give up on this whole thing if I'm going to rot down here in Egypt anyway!" But Joseph was able to make the best of everything, to use what he was given to its best advantage, and to allow God to worry about the results.

I learned that lesson from a man who was in a very successful position in his career. Things were going well; the people he worked with were happy; everything seemed to be rolling along smoothly. One day the head of the company came to him and asked him to take another position that both of them knew would be much more difficult than the work he was doing. It would also involve a move for his family and some major changes in their lifestyle. It was a hard decision. I saw him after he moved and asked how it was going. He said, "Jim, I've always figured that life is a whole lot like a boxing match. You go into the ring and do the best job you can do until somebody rings the bell. When he rings the bell, you leave that ring, go to the next one, and do the best job you can there, until somebody rings the bell. That's about the most that anybody can expect of you, and that's about enough to expect from yourself." He had learned how to do the best that he knew how to do with the situation that confronted him and leave the rest to the goodness and the purpose of God.

Corazon Aquino surprised the world. *Time* magazine acknowledged that "history is rarely a fairy tale, a narrative that instructs as well as inspires. Still less often is it a morality play, in which the forces of corruption and redemption . . . collide in perfect symmetry." But in 1986, as the rest of the world looked on in amazement and respect, the story of Corazon Aquino took on these qualities.

Ferdinand Marcos had called for elections. Who would run against him?

The widow of Marcos's most respected opponent discussed the decision with her advisers, family, and priest. Then she went for a spiritual retreat to a convent of the Sisters of Perpetual Adoration, just outside Manila. She had one free day, and she said she wanted to spend it in prayer. Here is how the reporter described the decision:

> Ten hours of meditation confirmed her in the earlier decision. "We had to present somebody who was the complete

opposite of Marcos," she said, "someone who has been a victim." She was modest but unflinching in her judgment of just who that person should be. "Looking around, I may not be the worst victim, but I am the best known."

With very little assurance of how the "fairy tale" would end, she took her role in the "morality play" being acted out in the islands. She ran against Marcos and won. She was not exaggerating when, two months after coming to power, she frankly declared, "I am not embarrassed to tell you that I believe in miracles." The secular writer defined the practical application of her faith:

> The absoluteness of that belief gives Aquino a firmness that can turn into stubbornness. . . . Faith is also the basis of her fatalism. "If someone wishes to use a bazooka on me," she once said, "it's goodbye. If it's my time to die, I'll go." Her sense of religion accounts too for Aquino's uncanny patience, her willingness, while awaiting what she regards as the appointed moment, to hold onto a burning match until it singes her fingers.

Richard Kessler, a senior associate for U.S.–Philippines relations at the Carnegie Endowment for International Peace, described her as "a very biblical type of person. . . . But it's not from a Hallmark card. It's saintliness as in the Old Testament."

Perhaps hers is the saintliness of an Old Testament character named Joseph, whose absolute belief in the purpose of God gave him firmness of character, and whose trust in God created an uncanny patience, the power to see it through.

CHAPTER THIRTEEN

How God Turns Evil into Good

I believe that God can and will bring good out of evil, even out of the greatest evil. For that purpose he needs men who make the best use of everything. I believe that God will give us all the strength we need to help us to resist in all time of distress. But he never gives it in advance, lest we should rely on ourselves and not on him alone. A faith such as this should allay all our fears for the future.

—Dietrich Bonhoeffer

READ GENESIS 45:1-8, 50:19-20

Time magazine called it "an unusual reunion," and that is exactly what it was. Forty years after the end of World War II, former German prisoners of war and their former captors reassembled in the tiny north woods village of Stark, New Hampshire, which had served as a stockade for two years during the war. They came back together for what the residents of Stark called "German-American Friendship Day," complete with brass bands, hot dogs, and speeches. The reporter said the men had a difficult time describing exactly what the event meant to them, not because of the difference in language but because "the ordinary formulas of memory and friendship did not quite fit."

The ordinary formulas do not quite fit the unusual reunion recorded at the end of the Book of Genesis, either. I tried to imagine how this event might have been reported in *The Nile Daily Times* or on the EGYPT-TV evening news. Perhaps it went something like this:

> November 23, 1750 B.C. An unusual reunion occurred today at the prime minister's residence. After a separation of twenty-two years, Joseph, second in command in the administration, was reunited with his eleven brothers, sons of a Hebrew shepherd from Canaan named Jacob, sometimes called Israel.
>
> Although the meeting was closed to the press, informed sources report that Joseph was separated from his brothers at the age of seventeen when they sold him to slave traders who brought him to Egypt. He served as a servant to Potiphar, the chief of the king's guards, but was imprisoned on charges of sexual harassment brought by Potiphar's wife. Those charges were never substantiated.
>
> Nine years ago he was released from prison and rose to power by interpreting the king's dreams and predicting the famine that is now in its second year. On his recommendation, the Federal Grain Reserve was formed, which has been credited with saving the nation from starvation.
>
> Even the prime minister's personal servants were excluded from the chamber, but reports are that it was a highly emotional reunion. Persons in the corridor could hear loud sobbing inside the room.
>
> The king has welcomed Joseph's family to Egypt and intends to allow them to settle in the grazing land of Goshen.

There are the facts. But a fact that is left out could be the

HOW GOD TURNS EVIL INTO GOOD

one to interpret all the rest. It is in the last words of Joseph. When he looks back across the years since he was carried off to Egypt, he tells his brothers, "You plotted evil against me, but God turned it into good, in order to preserve the lives of many people who are alive today" (50:20, TEV).

The central character in this drama is not a very good man named Joseph; the central character is a very good God who was able to take what had been intended for evil and use it for good—the God who turned defeat into salvation, the God who used the apparent death of Joseph to save the entire family and thereby to maintain the hope of the fulfillment of the covenant, the God who enabled Joseph to look back and say, "God sent me ahead of you . . . in this amazing way . . . to make sure that you and your descendants survive" (45:7, TEV).

St. Paul affirmed a similar quality of faith when he wrote, "We know that in all things God works for good with those who love him, those whom he has called according to his purpose" (Rom. 8:28, TEV).

Let me take a brief negative spree and share with you what I think these words do *not* mean. I am convinced that they do not mean many things like: "God always has a reason for everything" or "Don't worry; everything always works out for the best." A person is diagnosed as having terminal cancer; a co-worker falls over with a heart attack; a child runs in front of a drunken driver and is maimed or killed; a corporation reorganizes and people lose their jobs. When any of these things happen, some well-intentioned soul will step into the middle of personal suffering, fear, anxiety, and despair and philosophize, "Don't worry. God always has a reason for everything. Everything always works out for the best." Such individuals insist that God has absolute control over every circumstance and detail of every human being's life, as if God has a hand on every steering wheel and a finger on every destructive cell in every body, as if God manipulates every detail of human existence, as if God were responsible for everything that happens to us.

Joseph did not believe that. Neither did St. Paul. Neither did Peter, and as far as I can tell, neither did the early Christians. I do not believe it, either.

Joseph was looking directly into his brothers' eyes when he declared, "You intended this for evil." They chose to throw him into the pit. They decided to sell him into slavery. They plotted to go back and tell Jacob that his son had been killed by a wild animal. God did not force them to do any of those things. God did not cause what happened to Joseph. It was the result of human jealousy and pride, a consequence of the freedom that God has entrusted to the creation.

A huge percentage of the suffering, anxiety, fear, and despair surrounding us can be filed under one of two categories. One is the category of human choice and its consequences. The other is the category of the risky, dangerous freedom that God has written into the fabric of the universe. None of us is exempt from the risk and danger that are parts of the world in which we live. Situations exist in our lives that God does not appear to control. They are just things that happen, occurrences, events, circumstances that cross the path of our lives. But Joseph said, "Even though you meant it for evil, God turned it into good."

The good news is that while there may be circumstances over which God does not have absolute control and "things" that God does not cause, there is *no* thing that God cannot turn into good. God may not be the author of all things, but God is the master of all things. There is no event, no experience of human life, that God cannot somehow weave into the tapestry of God's good purpose for us. There is no accident or incident of human life that cannot become grist for the mill of God's redemptive purpose in our world and in our experience. There is no thing that God cannot use in some way for good. Paul says, "We know that in all things God works for good with those who love him, those whom he has called by his purpose."

Do not miss the structure of that sentence. *God* is the subject of the active verb: "God works." The King James translation reads, "All things work together for good." The problem is that "things" in and of themselves cannot "work" either for good or for evil. They are just "things," the raw material of experience. Joseph's faith, Paul's faith, and our faith are in the God who is the subject of the active verb, the creative God who brings order out of chaos.

Also, notice the prepositions. They are critical to our understanding of this verse. God works "*in* all things." God is here with us in the middle of all the events of our lives. God works "*for* good." God does not bring evil into lives of people. God always works for a good purpose. And God works "*with* those who love him." This life is a partnership, a cooperative project, a bold experiment in which both God and human beings have work to do. *In*, *for*, and *with* define the place, the purpose, and the process by which God is at work in human history.

We can see clearly what this faith meant for Joseph. It enabled him to look back across the years to the worst thing that ever happened to him and discover that in an amazing way, God used this suffering to preserve the people of Israel and to assure the continuation of the covenant. God took what was intended for evil and, in partnership with Joseph, turned it into good.

Do you want the all-time, awesome illustration of that truth? On the day of Pentecost, Peter preached the first Christian sermon. In the crowd were the people who had demanded the crucifixion of Jesus. To them, Peter declared, "This Jesus whom you crucified God raised from the dead" (Acts 2:23-24). God could even take the most horrendous choice, the most evil act in the history of humankind, and transform it into new life and hope.

"You meant it for evil, but God used it for good" means that God is at work in all things for good, in partnership with those who love God. And I wonder if we can begin to see our lives from that perspective. I wonder if we can begin to see all the incidents and accidents, all the circumstances and events that come into our experience through the perspective of faith, which dares to believe that although God may not have caused everything that comes our way, God is able to use anything for good, for hope, and for life.

Moorhead Kennedy reflects on his experience across 444 days as a hostage in Teheran in his book, *The Ayatollah in the Cathedral*. There are some strong parallels with the story of Joseph. One day their captors told the hostages they could write one letter home. Immediately the hostages assumed this meant they were going to be put to death in the very near future. Kennedy wrote this letter to his wife: "All of a sudden we have been told that we can write a letter. Whether this is just part of the considerably improved conditions that recently have been extended to us or whether this is a 'last letter' is not entirely clear. If it is the latter, I face it with unexpected serenity . . . I have no bitterness about anyone or anything. . . . If it is only the former then the experience I am going through will serve us both well." Kennedy's attitude seems very similar to the faith of Joseph in that he carried no bitterness and could envision some way in which every experience could be productive, could result in good.

One night one of Kennedy's roommates said out loud, "What have I done in my life to deserve this?"—which

HOW GOD TURNS EVIL INTO GOOD

must be the question Joseph often asked himself. Kennedy writes, "I was silent, but in my mind, I asked: Do you really believe that your past conduct has anything to do with it? You must imagine that, somewhere up there, there is a celestial judge, and a cosmic prosecutor, and a heavenly public defender! All you have to do is make your case. . . . As soon as the judge hears this, you'll be exonerated, and won't have to go through the hostage experience anymore. Why, I thought suddenly, we're all lucky to have been born."

Kennedy's wife, Louisa, writes the book's closing paragraphs, reflecting on what they learned through the experience. She said they discovered that the important thing is the quality, not the length, of human life, and knowing that life has been part of a purposeful plan. "Mike and I believe that to be part of the plan still allows the opportunity to make choices at certain forks in the road. By these choices we grow, we gain new dimensions. . . . Mike and I have made choices too. . . . There will be more. Katherine, Mike, and I, however, . . . are looking forward to a new and different life."

There is much more that could be said, that needs to be said, about these closing scenes in the life of Joseph. There is powerful human emotion here, revealed in a man who was strong enough to cry (42:24; 43:30; 45:2, 13-15; 46:29; 50:1, 17). There is suspense here as Joseph spins the web by which his identity is finally revealed and the entire family is brought back together. There is great hope for the future as Joseph asks his people to promise that when God leads them back to their homeland, they will take his body with them (50:25). But nothing stands out more powerfully in the unique witness of Joseph than his faith in the God who is at work in all things for good, in partnership with those who love God.

Joseph's affirmation is a fitting conclusion to the question, Where in the world is God? In the creation story we discovered that the underlying theme of the creation-Fall narrative is that God has neither abandoned the good purpose for the creation nor denied its freedom. We live in the crosscurrents of those two often-conflicting realities. God still intends good for this world and for our lives. God still longs, hopes, and works in our world to be able to say, "That's good!" But God has not abrogated the freedom of the created order. God did not deny the freedom of Joseph's brothers to sell him into slavery or the freedom of Potiphar's wife to have him thrown into prison. But beneath all the swirling currents of circumstances and change, the Creator is still at work to bring order out of chaos, to bring good out of evil, to bring life out of apparent death. God is able to take the evil choices, the bungling mistakes, the sinister circumstances of human existence and, in an amazing way, use them for good as a part of the fulfillment of the covenant.

The book of beginnings ends with the children of Israel far away from the Promised Land, but it ends with unbridled confidence in God's ability to work out the good purpose of the covenant in human history. Joseph's journey may end, but God's creative work in human history may just be beginning.

QUESTIONS FOR REFLECTION AND DISCUSSION

Introduction

1. How would you have responded to the question, "How can you believe in something you can't see?"

2. Have you ever had a personal experience which caused you to ask, "How can you believe in a good God in an evil world"? Share that experience with your group.

3. How do you respond to the affirmation that "Theology matters. The character of the God in whom we believe makes a gigantic difference in how we respond to the real experiences of life"? Can you find times when your understanding of God has influenced your response to specific situations?

4. How do you think it will affect your reading of the Book of Genesis if you see these as family stories told at an old-fashioned family reunion?

5. Share with your group at least one thing you hope will happen in your life as you journey with the people of Genesis. Make a list of the hopes that are shared by each member of the group and use them as an outline for prayer as you begin this study.

JOURNEYS WITH THE PEOPLE OF GENESIS
Chapter One: "Creation, Fall, and Then What?"

1. Where does the story of your life begin? Share briefly with the group your family "roots." Do you have anything in common with other persons in the group?
2. How do you respond to the statement, "The scientific approach that some Christians seem so intent to deny is leading others to a deeper faith"? Can you describe a time when this has happened for you?
3. What difference does it make for you to see the Book of Genesis as "the poetry of faith, the joyful cry of the soul to the God who brings order out of chaos"?
4. How do you define the difference between good and evil? How does the narrative of the Fall influence your understanding of these terms?
5. Central to our experience of the biblical narrative of creation and Fall is the concept of freedom. How do you feel about the comparison to the story of Pinocchio?
6. How do you reconcile the "constant tension between good and evil . . . the tug and pull of God's good purpose for the creation and the reality of evil around us"?

QUESTIONS FOR REFLECTION AND DISCUSSION
Chapter Two: "The Rainbow Connection"

1. Put yourself in Noah's place. How do you picture the morning after the flood?
2. Put yourself in God's place before the flood. Seeing the effects of the Fall, how would you have felt? What would you have done?
3. How do you respond to the statement, "God's wrath is an expression—not a contradiction—of goodness and grace. Its purpose is redemption, not destruction"?
4. How does Noah model the belief that "faithfulness and goodness are always possible, even in a world where everything and everyone seem to be driven by evil intent"?
5. What does the flood narrative say to you about the character of God?
6. Do you ever feel like Noah? Can you identify with the remnant of Israel in exile? How does this story help you in that experience?

JOURNEYS WITH THE PEOPLE OF GENESIS

Chapter Three: "Acting on the Promises"

1. If you could spend an evening with any one person, living, deceased, or fictional, whom would you choose and why?
2. If you had been Abraham, how would you have responded to God's invitation in Genesis 12:1-9?
3. How do you define *faith*? How do you react to faith in terms of acting on a new standard of measurement?
4. Who are the "Abrahams" in your life? Describe some person who has impressed you as a person who acted on the basis of his or her faith.
5. How would your lifestyle change as you acted on the belief that God's promise for your life will be fulfilled?

QUESTIONS FOR REFLECTION AND DISCUSSION
Chapter Four: "Strangely Blessed"

1. What image comes to your mind when you hear the word *blessed*?
2. What difference does it make for you to know that you have been blessed by God in order to be a blessing to the world?
3. Who are your heroes? Why?
4. Have you had times in your own experience when you knew that God was using your life as a blessing for someone else? How did it happen?
5. How do you respond to the stories of the "strangely blessed" persons that are told here? Can you see something in their lives that can be a model for your own witness?

JOURNEYS WITH THE PEOPLE OF GENESIS

Chapter Five: "Learning to Laugh with God"

1. Read Genesis 18:9-15 aloud from a contemporary translation. Discuss the frankness and humor of the story. Are you surprised by it?
2. Read aloud Frederick Buechner's description of Sarah. How does it make you feel? How does it help you understand the biblical story?
3. When was the last time you experienced the laughter of disbelief? Are there times when it is difficult for you to believe in the promises of God? How do you handle doubt?
4. How have you experienced the laughter of the surprising grace of God? When were you surprised by something good happening for you when you didn't expect it?
5. Do you have any problems with the image of God laughing? What difference does it make in your understanding of the personality and character of God?
6. Read (or sing) the Cowper hymn as a closing affirmation for your group.

QUESTIONS FOR REFLECTION AND DISCUSSION
Chapter Six: "The Road to Mount Moriah"

1. Have a member of the group read Genesis 22:1-19 as if it were a dramatic story being told to a listening audience. Discuss your feeling of the drama of it.
2. What is your initial response to this story? How does it make you feel?
3. Have you ever had times when you were forced to trust in the goodness of God even when the circumstances around you seemed to contradict that goodness? When? How did you cope with it?
4. Where have you experienced a "Mount Moriah"? What was God calling you to surrender?
5. With which of the three stories told at the conclusion of the chapter (the woman letter writer, the preacher's son, and C.S. Lewis) can you most clearly identify? Why?

Chapter Seven: "If You Don't Do It . . ."

1. How does the author's experience as a twin help you understand the story of Jacob and Esau?
2. Do you operate on the assumption that if you don't do it, it won't get done? How is that helpful? How is it harmful?
3. Are you surprised by the dishonesty of Jacob or the shallowness of Esau? How are they like us or different from us?
4. Have you ever been to Bethel, that place where you saw a ladder connecting heaven and earth, and knew that you were not alone? How have you discovered that the Lord is here with you?
5. Is there something in you that would rather attempt to do things by yourself than to allow God to be at work with you? How do you deal with that?

QUESTIONS FOR REFLECTION AND DISCUSSION

Chapter Eight: "Wrestling in the Dark, Limping Toward the Dawn"

1. Have you ever wished you could find a "new you"? How do you deal with the search for identity?
2. Have you ever been forced to deal with your past as Jacob was?
3. Can you identify with St. Paul's words in Romans 7:14-24? How have you faced that struggle?
4. How has your life become more complicated because of your faith?
5. Are there relationships that need to be restored in your life if you are to find the new identity God intends for you? What does it mean for you to live in a real world, a world with other people in it?
6. Is the emphasis on Jacob's limp and Jesus' scars a new idea for you? How has God used your "scars"? How has God used your weakness or failure for some good purpose?

JOURNEYS WITH THE PEOPLE OF GENESIS

Chapter Nine: "The Best Thing About Growing Old"

1. How do you feel about growing old?
2. How does the picture of Jacob returning to Bethel touch you? How do you identify with his journey?
3. Looking back across your own life, where are the places you can say, "Look at the way the Lord has helped us"?
4. Read the Addison hymn. Have you had moments like the worship service in Nairobi when you felt the kind of gratitude described here for God's mercy in your life?
5. Can you believe that God had something in mind for Jacob from the time he was born and worked with him to fulfill that identity? Can you believe it for yourself? What does this mean for you?

QUESTIONS FOR REFLECTION AND DISCUSSION
Chapter Ten: "Don't Forget Joseph"

1. Were you surprised by the contrast between the direct interaction of God in the first two-thirds of Genesis and the indirect presence of God in the story of Joseph? What does this say to you about the character of God?
2. Is it harder for you to believe in the "hiddenness" of God than to believe in the God who acts more directly?
3. Read the Lowell poem. Where have you experienced the hidden God who is silently at work in human history?
4. How have you experienced the assurance that God's purpose will triumph in spite of contradictory circumstances?
5. What difference does the story of Joseph make in your faith?

JOURNEYS WITH THE PEOPLE OF GENESIS

Chapter Eleven: "Here Comes the Dreamer!"

1. Who have you known who found inner strength for their lives because they were possessed by a dream?
2. How does Martin Luther King's "I Have A Dream" speech impress you? How did you feel the first time you heard it?
3. What dreams motivate your life?
4. What keeps your dreams alive over the long haul?
5. Share some experience that touched your life the way the Peter, Paul and Mary concert touched the author's life.

QUESTIONS FOR REFLECTION AND DISCUSSION
Chapter Twelve: "The Power to See It Through"

1. How does the character of Don Quixote impress you?
2. Have you experienced the emotional rollercoaster described by Will Steger on the way to the North Pole?
3. Make a chart or line graph with the story of Joseph, tracking the ups and downs of his experience. How would you have responded to this kind of life?
4. Where does a person find the strength to maintain his or her integrity in temptation?
5. Have you known anyone who, like Joseph, continued to trust God under difficult circumstances? Tell that person's story.
6. How do you respond to the story of Corazon Aquino?

JOURNEYS WITH THE PEOPLE OF GENESIS

Chapter Thirteen: "How God Turns Evil into Good"

1. Have you ever experienced an "unusual reunion" like the one described at the beginning of this chapter?
2. Who do you understand to be the central character in this drama? How is God active here?
3. Read Romans 8:28 in several different translations of scripture. How do you apply that affirmation to your own life experience?
4. Do you agree with the author's conviction that a huge degree of human suffering comes from either human choice or "the risky, dangerous freedom that God has written into the fabric of the universe"?
5. How does the story of Joseph relate to the creation narrative with which the Book of Genesis begins?
6. How has your understanding of God changed during this journey through Genesis?

ABOUT THE AUTHOR

James A. Harnish is the Pastor of St. Luke's United Methodist Church at Windermere in Orlando, Florida, a congregation he helped to organize in 1979. He has also served other churches in Florida and is actively involved in the civic and religious lives of his community. He and his wife Marsha are the parents of two daughters, Carrie Lynn and Deborah Jeanne.

Mr. Harnish's previous books include *Jesus Makes the Difference!* and *What Will You Do With King Jesus?*